WHAT COLOR IS YOUR PARACHUTE?

FOR COLLEGE

WHAT COLOR IS YOUR PARACHUTE?
FOR COLLEGE

PAVE YOUR PATH FROM
MAJOR TO **MEANINGFUL WORK**

KATHARINE BROOKS

TEN SPEED PRESS
California | New York

Contents

Part 1

PREPARING FOR DEPARTURE: PACK YOUR BACKPACK FOR THE TRIP

This section will help you acquire the self-knowledge and resiliency to successfully navigate the job search.

Part 2

TAKE OFF: PARACHUTE INTO YOUR FUTURE

This section will help you develop your plans and design the communications to connect you to your future.

Part 3

LAND: FIND A DESTINATION THAT FITS

This section will help you land safely and securely in a future that fits.

Introduction

You, the Job Search, and This Book

———

Ashley, a college senior, is concerned about her friends. Everyone is stressed. Some are in suits and interviewing almost daily with prestigious banks or consulting firms. They seem so sure of themselves, like they have their futures all worked out. And yet she's heard their worried conversations in the hallways before classes. They ask themselves if they really know what they're doing. Are they just doing it to please their parents? And what if they don't get a job after all this work?

Other friends have different worries. They don't even own suits, and they wonder if something is wrong. Shouldn't they be doing something to find a job? But what? They worry that it's too late. That they've missed the best opportunities—and the job market isn't stable. They are always comparing themselves to others, sometimes feeling a temporary relief ("at least my major is more marketable" . . .), other times feeling more anxious ("I wish I had done an internship like she did" . . .).

But Ashley's not stressed. And she's not worried that she's missing out by not interviewing on campus. A psychology major, she is also studying banjo with one of the finest banjo players in the world. You might think she'd be caught in that classic career dilemma: should she follow a passion or be practical? But she's not. She likes both subjects equally, and she's making no effort to choose.

She has applied for several post-graduate scholarships that will allow her to study developmental neuroscience in London while playing her

1

banjo in the pubs on the weekend. She's hoping to start a band while she's there. The coronavirus has postponed her plans for the semester, but she's excited about moving to England when she can, and she's not forcing herself into a mold of what she's supposed to be or do. Who knows where being a banjo-playing neuropsychologist might end up?

• • •

So why isn't Ashley worried about the job search like everyone else? Because she knows a secret: she knows herself. She knows what her interests and skills are, and she knows how she wants to apply them. She knows the kind of life she wants, and she knows how to pursue it. And she already has a back-up plan if none of the scholarships comes through. Thanks to using the time-honored yet modern system in this book, she is confident she will end up creating her own interesting job and life. You will, too.

If you're reading this book, you are probably a college student. And you're likely concerned about your future.

You might be enrolled in:

- a traditional four-year college or university
- a community college pursuing a specific vocational program
- a community college looking to transfer to a four-year school
- a graduate or professional school
- high school and taking lots of advanced placement college-level courses
- an online degree program while you work full-time or are in the military

And you might be thinking (or worrying) about:

- what to major in
- finding an internship
- finding a summer job
- what career field to pursue
- what the job market will look like when you graduate
- what the long-lasting economic effect of the coronavirus will be
- whether to start your own business
- whether to go to graduate school
- whether to go to law school or medical school

But no matter what degree or future you're pursuing, you are probably a busy, overwhelmed, stressed student looking for the best way to find a job you will love, no matter what the job market looks like. Let this book be your guide.

What Color Is Your Parachute? for College is based on the excellent work of Richard Bolles, who wrote the first edition of *What Color Is Your Parachute?* in the 1970s and introduced the most popular, successful, and bestselling job-hunting system in the world. And now it is presented and modified for you, a college student.

The image of the parachute is particularly appropriate for your situation. You know what a parachute is, of course: it's a circular cloth that catches the wind like a sail and helps you land safely on the ground.

This book has been written with that purpose in mind; to help you catch the wind like a sail and land safely into your new job, career, or life. To have an easy flight to a future that fits, in whatever way you define "fit." The Parachute System is divided into three parts. You start by Preparing for Departure and packing your Backpack, which will give you all the substance and confidence you need. You Take Off, setting up conversations (social media, networking, and interviewing) and choosing and connecting to potential interesting landing sites. Finally, armed with new knowledge about yourself and all the opportunities out there, you Land safely in your desired setting.

So is this a "job" book or a "career" guide? Well, it's both. The words will be used interchangeably throughout the book. In some respects, the "job" is just the current position you're in, whereas the "career" represents the totality of your work. Since you're just starting out, you will be looking at both. You might just need a job—but that job might also be the start of a career. Or not. It might just be the job you get while you look for a different one. That's okay, because that's how careers are born, and that's why we talk about "transferable skills." The skills you develop in your job might lead you to a totally new career. Your job goals will change as your career interests change and vice versa. What's most important is that you will learn from it. Whatever your job, you will learn what you like and what you don't like, and you will use that job as a launching pad for the next.

Richard Bolles describes the job search as a Neanderthal process, and he's right. It is filled with strange activities: talking to strangers and calling it "networking"; answering odd questions at interviews, like "Why are manhole covers round?"; and writing archaic documents such as resumes and cover letters.

But did you know the college job search is uniquely different from other job searches?

- College students have certain advantages: you have unique access to career guidance and employers who come to your campus. You have a large network of alumni who want to help you just because you're going to the school they graduated from. And you have the label of "student," which means people are more likely to assist you because they want to help.

- But maybe you're trying to do this job search while you're also dealing with your already-busy life of papers, exams, projects, grades, classes, activities, work, and social events. And you're likely feeling a sense of urgency about the process. College students often feel immense pressure to figure out what to do, how to do it, where to do it, and to do it quickly. The hot careers of the moment—investment banking and consulting—seem to drive this pace at many colleges, easily skewing your perceptions of the job market.

- To add to the pressure, sometimes it feels like this search is about everyone else: what your parents or family would like you to do, what your roommate or friends are doing, what employers want from you. That's a lot of people to please. Not to mention a lot of expectations to live up to.

- And the job market itself can be wildly unpredictable, as students who graduated in 2020 learned when the coronavirus pandemic swept the world and changed the unemployment rate from 3.6 percent in January of 2020 to over 13 percent in May. Job market fluctuations can make it hard to plan your future.

- And maybe, just maybe, you are a perfectionist and you push yourself to find the perfect job, no matter what others say.

So let's stop for a moment. Take a breath. Think of your favorite teachers. What made them the best? They believed in you, right? They knew you could do whatever task they assigned. They gave you hope and support and the knowledge that you can accomplish anything. And they guided you along the way. That's what Richard Bolles does in his books. And that's what you're going to find here: hope, a guide, someone who believes in you. Someone who has a ton of experience guiding students just like you to find amazing career opportunities. Someone who will help you move forward with less stress and more fun.

Tyler returned to campus to talk to students about his two post-graduate internships in Hollywood. He told the students about his struggle to decide on a career, but that he is now committed to film-making. "How did you know you were committed to filmmaking?" a student asked. Tyler thought for a minute and said, "It was the moment I decided to submit my films to festivals for judging." Previously he had just thought about promoting his films, but he hadn't taken any action. By submitting his films to festivals, he knew he had to make the best product he could. And suddenly he found a whole new world of connections in the industry. He has had lots of conversations, honed his craft, learned to take criticism and advice, and is now finding his "tribe" in the workplace. And jobs. Lots of them.

• • •

With this book, you now have the same choice. This is the moment you, too, can commit to designing your future. Not by worrying about it. Not by focusing on what other people are doing, or what other people want you to do, but by giving yourself the time and mental space to do the exercises and Thought Organizers that will help you explore yourself, the many options you have, and the steps you can take to get where you want to go.

Make no mistake: job hunting isn't simple. It isn't easy. It's particularly challenging when the unemployment rate is high. It's easy to feel overwhelmed. But if you use this system and take it step by step, you will succeed. You will avoid the emotional and actual problems your friends have encountered, and you will move toward whatever future you have defined for yourself. The Parachute System that you will learn through the exercises in this book is tried-and-true. It works when the economy is great, and it works when the economy is not so great. No matter what the job market looks like when you graduate, this system will support you.

Doing the many exercises in *What Color Is Your Parachute? for College* requires time and commitment. But the exercises will be interesting, so the time should fly by, and you will learn so much about yourself and the life you want to live. So take a step back from the pressure you're feeling. Relax and have fun doing the exercises in whatever order works for you. Try out the suggested activities. Learn and grow from the feedback you'll receive and you, too, will be a pro at the job search.

Career development never ends. It's a constant exploration, a journey if you will, and you get to set the parameters that work for you. You get to decide how long to stay on a job, in a career field, or even in an industry. You have your choice of destinations. This book is designed to help you both narrow down and increase your choices. It will help you expand your thinking and come up with new and better ideas about your future and your plans.

We're going to start with you. Not the job market, not what's hot, not what your roommate is doing or your friends are doing. Start with you. Focus on what you enjoy.

As Richard Bolles writes, "It's on you. You are the hero of this book."

- What do you want?
- What's important to you?
- What kind of work are you hoping to find?
- What kind of life do you want to create?

Let's get started.

Thought Organizers and How to Use This Book

This book is about you: your ideas, your vision, your creativity, your thoughts. And it's a book, so the first step is to read it. You can just read it through if you wish, but you'll get much more out of it if you do the exercises. Writing everything down greatly increases the likelihood that you will remember all your brilliant insights and ideas.

Many of the exercises are called "Thought Organizers" because that's just what they do. They help you take your random ideas and thoughts and put them in a format that makes them easy to see. They not only organize your thoughts, they help clarify your plans, simplify the job search, and save you time. They will also help you remember what's important about yourself and the future you're seeking.

These Thought Organizers are simple shapes (lines, lists, squares, circles, etc.) you can easily re-create anywhere—on your computer or even on a napkin at your favorite coffee shop. What's important is that you do them, and you have a place to store them. Set up a system on your computer as well as in a notebook or another paper filing system. That way you can use whatever works best at a given moment. Consider using an app, like Trello, to organize your search process. Some quick suggestions for powering through this system:

- **Consider everything you write a possibility.** But not a rule or a requirement, the goals you set might not work. Reset them. You might change your mind. Keep your plans flexible and update them regularly. The job search can be a fast-moving process; even when you think you know what is going to happen, you might be surprised.

- **Adopt the GPS tracker as your metaphor.** When you make a wrong turn or an unexpected stop, what does it do? It recalibrates with no judgment. You can recalibrate, too, any time you want.

- **Bring a friend along.** Richard Bolles had a great philosophy about the job search. He called it "Each one, teach one." Make a commitment with a friend to read a chapter and then meet up for coffee to do the exercises together. Learn from each other. Or make a commitment to read a chapter and then teach the chapter. Do the activities and then help another student do the activities. You will learn so much more, and you've helped someone else along the way. How's that for a great potential interview story?

PART 1

Preparing for Departure

PACK YOUR BACKPACK FOR THE TRIP

This section will help you acquire the self-knowledge and resiliency to successfully navigate the job search.

Start Off Strong

Challenges, Majors, and a Plan

Kayla just arrived on campus and she's already caught in a whirlwind of orientation activities. One of her required sessions is with the career center. "Seriously?" she's thinking. "I just got here and they want to talk about what I'll do when I leave? I'd just like to know where the dining hall is." But she goes, because she has to, listens to a list of services and makes a mental note that someday, one day, she'll think about that. Because right now, she's got way too many other things on her mind.

• • •

Does this sound familiar? Have you felt overwhelmed almost since you arrived? Maybe you never followed up on that plan to visit the career center in your first semester? That's okay. While it's important for you to know that the center is there and will help you, it's fine to focus on more immediate needs such as the dining hall and your classes.

That said, there are some decisions you'll need to make relatively early in your time in college, and starting to think about possible career options can be helpful. This chapter will help you identify and reduce those common stressors in college and in the job search and help you make some early critical decisions.

Overcoming Challenges in College and With the Job Search

Part of landing safely in your future involves staying healthy and keeping your stress level down, no matter what is happening in the world. Let's take a look at some of the internal challenges you might be facing, not only in college but also in your job search.

EXPECTATIONS

Expectations equal pressure. Does it feel like everyone has a plan for you? Maybe you're not only expected to do well in your classes but everyone says you need to build your resume by participating in all sorts of activities, doing internships, getting great summer jobs, and more.

- Maybe you're trying to fulfill family expectations—everyone from your great-grandfather on has been an attorney so you're expected to do the same.
- Maybe you're the first in your family to go to college, and now everyone's looking at you to succeed and achieve. You don't want to let anyone down, right?
- What expectations might you be placing on yourself?
- Are you a perfectionist who always has to hit the mark?
- Have you always been the "science superstar," and now you're facing much more difficult science courses in college?
- Are you trying hard to fit in or joining lots of groups to be popular or just more social?

Taking note of the expectations you're experiencing is important when you start thinking about your career choices.

COMPARISONITIS

Yes, comparisonitis is a thing. With social media and lots of attention placed on winning—however that's defined—the pressure to do better and be better is nonstop. It's all about looking good. It's easy to look around and see what your fellow students are doing and then compare yourself to them favorably or not. It's like everyone has a ruler out, and they're measuring the differences between themselves and others, feeling great if they are doing better, but feeling defeated if they're not. It's hard to focus on yourself and enjoy your life when you're busy watching others. But if your focus is on what careers other students are pursuing, you aren't focusing on *your* career choices.

FEAR OF MISSING OUT

Related to comparisonitis, fear of missing out can leave you feeling like you can never relax. Relaxing is dangerous because you might miss something. You constantly worry that past decisions were mistakes. You have this ongoing undercurrent of concern that there is something you should have done, or should be doing now.

FEELING OVERWHELMED

Too much stuff, right? Just too many assignments, too many new friends, too many parties or distractions, too many interests. And now you're supposed to find this great internship or job. It's easy to feel overwhelmed, particularly if you tend to be introverted or shy. All the newness and group-living situations can make you feel like you need to find a cave somewhere and hide. Despite what you might think, you're definitely not alone. Pretty much everyone is feeling overwhelmed despite the images they project.

IMPOSTER SYNDROME

Do you ever feel like you don't belong, or you don't have the "proper" background to be where you are? Like someone made a big mistake in hiring you or selecting you for a special program or honor? You are not the only one. Career centers hear this concern almost daily. When complimented on a recent internship they completed, students say, "Oh anyone could have gotten it." Or when asked to talk about awards they received, "Oh, I was just lucky that day." They express uncertainty as in, "Am I really good enough?" You are. You belong.

PERSONAL CHALLENGES

Concerns unique to your situation can crop up: financial pressures or personal issues such as a disability, a sexual orientation, or a mental health challenge. These can leave you feeling adrift and unsupported. Maybe even your personality type (a tendency to procrastinate or be a perfectionist, for example) works against you as to try to navigate your way through college.

It's important for you to identify the potential challenges you might be facing, even if they're not mentioned above. Let's start a Thought Organizer of the challenges you're currently facing or focused on. Just fill in the challenges you're feeling right now.

Challenges Thought Organizer

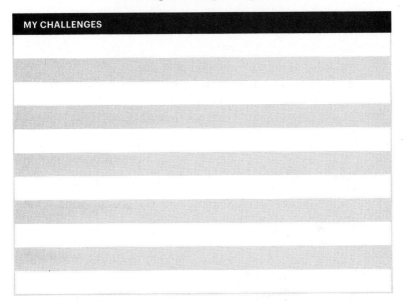

MY CHALLENGES

Before we start tackling those challenges, stop a moment. And congratulate yourself. Because, despite those challenges, here you are. In college. Succeeding. No matter what has held you back or has the potential to hold you back, here you are and you're fine. It's okay. And not only is it okay, there are concrete steps you can take to overcome your challenges. Here are ten ways.

1 **Know that you are not alone.** I can't tell you how many students start their conversations with, "I know this is weird" . . . or "I know this problem is unique" . . . but it's not. Believe me, 99 percent of what you are going through, someone else has experienced. People who have felt "all alone" with their troubles often find new friends and support when they just have the courage to admit to their challenges. If nothing else, the #MeToo movement has demonstrated that. Just by saying "me too" you are now part of group that understands you and knows what you have gone through.

2   **Don't be afraid to ask for help.** Colleges have all sorts of services set up to help you through whatever challenge you're facing. Whether it's:

- the **career center** to help with your future plans;
- a **well-being program** to help manage stress;
- an **advising office** (or adviser) to help decide on your classes;
- an **LGBTQ+ office** to provide affirmation, support, and information;
- a **counseling center** to help with mental health issues;
- a **diversity center** to offer empathy, acceptance, and cultural understanding;
- a **writing center** to help with your papers;
- a **financial aid office** for financial support and guidance; or
- a **tutoring center** to help get through those tough classes

the support you need is there. These people want to help you. Think about this: *the college employs people whose jobs depend on you seeking their help.* Even if you're a little shy about approaching one of these offices, remember, you're helping to keep them employed! And—they will care about you. It never hurts to know that someone cares, particularly when you are feeling alone with your challenges.

3   **Practice self-compassion.** Sometimes we think that by being hard on ourselves we will perform better. But that's not what Dr. Kristin Neff at The University of Texas has found. She has discovered that self-compassion can actually improve your motivation and performance.[1]

Do you want to lift yourself up or put yourself down? If you don't support yourself, who will? You are the only one who knows exactly what pressures you are feeling, and you can be the start of your own support group. Not sure how to do that? Here are some ideas to get you started:

- Be kind to yourself.
- Say nice things when you talk to yourself.
- Is what you are telling yourself really true?
- Would there be enough evidence for it to stand up in a courtroom?
- Would a supportive friend say that to you?
- When you catch yourself saying something less than helpful, ask yourself if you would say the same thing to a friend.

Self-compassion includes taking care of yourself, recognizing when you need support and help, and then seeking it out. It also involves accepting what happens without judging it negatively, and recognizing that negative experiences are part of the normal human condition. Simple actions such as keeping a nightly gratitude journal can help remind you of what is good in your life. Reminding yourself of the times when you have faced challenges and prevailed can help. Remember that "imposter syndrome" mentioned earlier? That's just self-doubt. If you completed an internship or you received an award, someone thought you deserved it. Who are you to argue with their wisdom? Keep reminding yourself, "I belong here." Read on to start practicing self-compassion right now!

4 **Have a growth mindset.** Carol Dweck's excellent book *Mindset: The New Psychology of Success* points out the value of always being a learner. People who have a growth mindset view failure as an opportunity to improve and to learn. They use challenges to grow. They look at what successful people they admire do and then model them. They are curious and seek out new information and new experiences. Conversely, people with fixed mindsets tend to be hard on themselves and give up easily. They assume that their skills are fixed; if they're not good at something now, they never will be. This type of mindset can cause you to take fewer risks, avoid challenging or new situations, and give up quickly, thus reinforcing your negative view of yourself. Read Dr. Dweck's book to learn even more and try to catch when you might be caught up in a fixed mindset.

5 **Develop an optimistic mindset.** It's easy to get caught up in negativity and complaining, particularly if your friends or family tend to react this way to life situations. But research has shown that we can adapt new frames for how we view people and situations, and those new frames can help us be more positive and more resilient. Generally, optimistic people have been found to be more successful in many careers, including teaching, sales, and management. Simply focusing on the good in a situation can help. If you'd like to learn more about how to adopt a more optimistic attitude and lifestyle, check out Dr. Martin Seligman's positive psychology website and take the tests related to learned optimism. Learn what your current level of optimism is and learn some tricks for improving it.

6 Set goals for your future—create a call to action. If you're feeling like you have a million things to do, try writing down those "to-do's" and turning them into goals. The mere act of creating a list (a Thought Organizer, as we like to call it) can help you feel back in control. Getting all those pressures out of your head and onto a piece of paper can start to make them more manageable. In his book *The Seven Habits of Highly Effective People,* author Stephen Covey talks about the "big rocks" in our lives. These are the major tasks or parts of our lives that we must take care of, even if they aren't pressing at the moment. (Want to learn more about the big rocks in your life? Go to YouTube and look for Covey's big rocks videos. He does a great demonstration that will help you think more clearly about your priorities.)

So let's make some lists.

- What are your big rocks: the big items you need to stay focused on?

  – The classes you are taking or want to take.
  – The careers you'd like to consider.
  – The clubs or organizations you'd like to join.
  – The other responsibilities you have, such as a work-study job or volunteer activities.
  – Your friends and fun activities.
  – Taking care of children or family members who are ill.

Just making lists can help you decide which items you want to move to your to-do list, and which are just nice ideas that you can't do right now, so you can stop pressuring yourself to do them. Decide which items you will move forward on and let the others go.

What is your call-to-action for tomorrow? That's all you have to think about. Just tomorrow. And then the next day. And then the next.

Let's try this right now. What list could you create that would help you feel calm and more in control? Get out your notebook and draw this Thought Organizer on your paper.

BIG ROCK #1	BIG ROCK #2	BIG ROCK #3	BIG ROCK #4
Name	Name	Name	Name
To-do's	**To-do's**	**To-do's**	**To-do's**

Here's a sample.

BIG ROCK #1	BIG ROCK #2	BIG ROCK #3	BIG ROCK #4
Classes	Organizations	Work-Study Job	Career Planning
To-do's • Paper for English class due Friday • Test in chemistry next Tuesday • Reading for history class tomorrow	**To-do's** • Go to tonight's meeting • Set up committee • Create new member reception	**To-do's** • Organize the lab • Inventory the supplies • Talk to admin about ordering materials	**To-do's** • Visit the career center during drop-ins this week • Start resume • Talk about career ideas

Once you have identified all the big items in your life and have jotted down your list of "to-do's" you can create a master list of what you want to do in the next twenty-four hours. Just taking your list one day at a time can help you start to feel in control.

Here are some other ways to organize your "to-do's":

• Consider creating the list structure (the columns) on a large piece of paper or a whiteboard and then use sticky notes to write each of the "to-do's." You can then move them around if you need to change the order or remove them when you complete them.

• Prefer to use your computer? Set up a Trello account (it's free) and put your goals and plans on that.

No matter what system you use, you will find it mentally relaxing to get everything out of your head and onto paper or a device. You will start to feel like everything is more manageable.

7 **Sleep, eat, play, and relax.** It's amazing how quickly stress and pressure can disrupt our schedules. You suddenly realize it's 5:00 p.m. and you never got lunch. Or you have a paper due tomorrow, and the only time available to write it is between midnight and 5:00 a.m. So there you are.

Food isn't just what you eat; think about spiritual food. What do I need to feel fulfilled? What is important to me right now? Am I focusing on that? Or am I more worried about what other people are thinking?

Use whatever works to keep you healthy. Make it a goal: "Every day, I will do something to make me healthier or more centered."

That might mean visiting the gym; eating vegetables, fruit, and protein; watching a meditation video on YouTube; spending time outside; or taking a yoga class. The list can be endless, but to make it successful, select what *you* would enjoy and what *you* need. What works for one person might not work for another.

So what will help you relax? How can you detach from the craziness even if just for 10 or 30 minutes? What will help you feel more centered? Make another list and post it someplace where you will see it often. When you're getting stressed, just look at the list and pick one of the ideas that would be helpful.

Healthy Option Thought Organizer

MY HEALTHY OPTIONS
Yoga
Running
Watching my favorite TV show
Dance
Mediation
Friends
Music and singing
Writing
Calling home
Calling my friends at other schools
Texting a friend
Practicing my religion

8 **Preserve stability.** When you start your job search activities, you might find you're neglecting other activities. In your effort to write your resume, you might be behind on a paper. When you think about your future plans, you may start to lose your focus on your classes. As much as possible, keep everything else the same in your life as you explore your career options. Keep going to your student group meetings, keep up with your friendships, and, most important, keep up with your classes. Your job search doesn't have to take all your time. By spacing out the various activities, you can keep your job search manageable and fun. That's a promise. You have lots of time while you're in college to explore your future. Take small bites at a time throughout all four years.

9 Harness the power of the word "yet." This is my favorite strategy for dealing with all those things you know you need to do but haven't done. And all your frustrations around what you want and what isn't happening in your life (yet). What does "yet" mean? Well, yet means hope. It says, "I don't have a resume . . . *yet.*" "I haven't found an internship . . . *yet.*" "I don't know what career I want to pursue . . . *yet.*" The word "yet" implies that it will come. Hopefully in the near future. You don't have to worry about what you haven't done, because you will do it. Maybe tonight. Maybe next week. Set a goal. Set a date. But know it's okay if you haven't done it because well, you just haven't done it . . . yet. Try making a list of what you haven't done yet:

The Yet Thought Organizer

MY YET LIST: WHAT I PLAN TO DO

Your "yet" list is a great place to keep all the "coulda shoulda woulda" items that you know you want or need to do in the future but aren't quite ready to tackle them. You can always refer back to the list when you have a spare hour and decide which item you want to tackle.

10 Keep it fun. Look for ways to keep the job search interesting and enjoyable. In the same ways you want a future that fits, you also want your job-search method to fit. Adjust your job search to fit your personality. If you tend to be introverted or love research, put those skills to work by using the internet to find out as much as possible about your career. If you are a people-person, use LinkedIn and your alumni database to find potential connections with people who can help you find internships and jobs. Go to networking events at your school.

The chapters in this book will help you with all aspects of your search, but always keep your personal style in mind. As much as possible, draw on your strengths while also finding new skills. Try not to turn the job search into one more chore, one more expectation, one more pressure on yourself. It's in the title of this book: *What Color is Your Parachute?* Not your parents' parachute, or your friends' parachutes, or your professor's parachute. It's yours. So don't make decisions just to please others. If everyone in your family has been in a particular career field and you like that field, too, well that's great. Go for it. But if you don't like that field, and you have something else in mind, then go for that. It won't be fun if you're fulfilling someone else's expectations for you.

A Plan For Tackling Your Challenges

Now that you've discovered some possible coping mechanisms, revisit the Challenges list you created on page 13. The mere act of listing your challenges and then your possible solutions or remedies can help you relax. You're handling it. That's all that matters. You're now in a mental space of possibilities, of potential. That's all you can ask of yourself. So try listing some possible solutions or coping techniques you might want to try.

Coping with Challenges Thought Organizer

MY CHALLENGES	MY PLAN FOR COPING OR OVERCOMING

Did you have trouble coming up with solutions? Then it's time to get other people's opinions. As a popular motivational quote says, "You can't solve a problem with the same mindset that created it." (The quote is often attributed to Albert Einstein but not authenticated.) You might need the help of a different mind to find the best solution, particularly if your previous attempts at solving the challenge haven't succeeded. Just know that you're not alone with whatever might be challenging you. *Seek help.* The best students do.

Your First Major Decision

One of the most important decisions you will face when you enroll in college is what to major in. For instance, did you know that one of the best ways to reduce the cost of college is to graduate on time? And part of the secret of graduating on time is selecting a major as early in the process as possible and monitoring any changes you make, like adding a minor or an additional major. Here are some tips to help you with your decision:

- Take a look at your college catalog and note the deadline for declaring your major. Some schools require you to declare before you enroll, others allow you to wait until the end of your sophomore year.

- If you have a major in mind, declare it as soon as possible. Certain programs, such as music, engineering, accounting, chemistry, and physics often require more classes for the major and require you to start immediately in your first semester. Other majors (history, English, Latin American studies, and other liberal arts fields of study) might have fewer required courses so you have more flexibility as to when to declare your major. Every school is different, so be sure to check your college catalog. Keep in mind that declaring a major early might get you access to upper-level courses earlier than nonmajors.

- Read the requirements for your major and make sure that you begin taking the courses you will need, also known as prerequisites. For instance, many economics programs require that you start by taking micro and macroeconomics before you can take any more economics courses. The earlier you can schedule the prerequisites the better.

- At the same time, don't stress about delaying your major decision. Many colleges require a certain number of hours in a range of introductory classes—the sciences, foreign languages, social sciences, literature, and so on. Sometimes these are called "distribution courses" or "core courses." Your advisor can help you identify these courses. While you're still exploring ideas about majors, start taking these courses right away so you can eliminate those requirements early—and you might just find a new subject you love.

- According to The National Center for Educational Statistics, as cited by CNBC.com,[2] the six most popular majors are business, health professions, social sciences and history, psychology, biology/biomedical sciences, and engineering.

- If you ask the internet for a list of the "best" majors you will invariably be led to the majors that have the most earning potential (usually business and engineering and pre-medical related majors). So if all you are interested in is making money, that may be your best pathway as well. In their College Salary Report, PayScale offers a list of salaries by major. However, if you're interested in making the world a better place, PayScale also ranks majors by meaningfulness.[3] Their survey indicates that people enrolled in health science majors rated their work higher in meaning than people enrolled in business majors. So the "best" major has a lot more to do you with you than some survey.

What is the best major for you? Let's start with a quick self-assessment—which of these boxes best fits you:

1	2	3	4	5
I have no idea what to major in or what I want to do in the future.	I don't know what I'm majoring in, but I think I know what I want to do in the future.	I have several ideas about what to major in and I also have several ideas about my future.	I know exactly what I'm majoring in but not sure what I want to do in the future.	I know exactly what I'm majoring in and where I will apply it in the future.

Did you give yourself a "5" and think you can now skip this section? Don't. Not yet. Before you move on from this section, take just a few minutes to answer the following questions:

1 Have you met the professors in the department, and are they teaching interesting courses?
2 Do you like the classes you'll be enrolled in?
3 Have you gone to the bookstore and reviewed the many textbooks you'll be reading over the next few years? Are they interesting to you? Are you curious to learn more about the subjects they cover?
4 Have you decided whether to also pursue a minor or a second major? Why or why not? What would your likely choice be?

Even if you're sure about your major and career, double-check your decision by doing the Meta-Major Fair Exercise on page 26 and do the Four-Year Thought Organizer at the end of this chapter.

Now, for those of you who checked boxes 1 to 4, let's dig a little more.

What's most important to you about your major? Here are some common student responses:

- My major needs to be something I'm really interested in.
- My major needs to be very practical—something I can directly apply to a job.
- I have a specific skill I want to hone (for example, creative writing or a foreign language), and I need a major that will help me do that.
- My major needs to focus on something meaningful to me. I want to apply what I learn to make a better world.
- My major needs to be lucrative, I want to earn a lot of money using the knowledge from my major.
- My major needs to be relatively easy, I don't want to work all that hard to get through college.
- I want to major in something my friends are majoring in.
- I want a major that doesn't require a lot of writing. I don't like papers.
- I want a major that doesn't require a lot of math. I don't like math.
- I want a major with few requirements, so I have time for a second major or several minors.

WHAT'S IMPORTANT TO YOU IN A MAJOR

As you think about your major choice, here are five key thoughts to keep in mind:

1 **What do you want to learn?** This is perhaps the most important question to ask yourself. You will be immersing yourself in a very specific body of knowledge over your time in college. What would you most like to be informed about? What would you like to specialize in? What academic or professional "niche" would you like to build expertise in?

2 You are not choosing a career. Did you know that only 27 percent of college graduates work in fields directly related to their majors?[4] In fact, humanities, business, and even STEM students all end up in the same fields. Truth is, we waste too much time trying to match majors to careers. Of course, if you know what you want for a future career, and it requires a specific degree (like accounting or engineering), by all means, pursue that major. But for the rest of you, you will have career flexibility with most majors. Careers such as sales, marketing, management, business, and finance are open to all majors. Your focus should be on the skills and competencies you acquire in and out of the classroom. In fact, coming into a field from a "different" major can be a benefit because you bring a new perspective to the conversation. Your goal is to demonstrate how your major, along with your talents, skills, interests, expertise, and values make you the perfect candidate for the right position. And that's what this whole book is about.

3 Major in what you enjoy. I have worked with incredibly focused and happy engineering students. They love what they are learning in their classes, and they lose track of all hours figuring out a solution to a mechanical problem. I've also met just as many who aren't happy at all. They are surviving. They have followed the curriculum usually because someone else told them to, or because everyone says it will lead to a lucrative job. And if that's enough for you, then go for the lucrative job or major that leads to it. But if you can, pause for a moment and think about what major would be more fulfilling.

4 Be willing to change your major if needed. Your college curriculum has probably introduced you to new subjects. And it's okay to change your mind based on your new knowledge. Some students tell me they regret that they stuck with whatever major they selected while in high school. They had told their parents and friends they were going to be "X" (a doctor, a lawyer, a musician) and they pursued the major that fit. They aren't as sure about that now, but they are afraid to go back on their word. What will everyone say? It's scary to leave a path you thought was secure, but if your plans have changed, your path may need to change, too. Here's where a conversation with your academic advisor can be helpful. You just might find that changing your major will open a new world for you.

5 Keep an open mind about your potential. Just because you didn't like a subject in high school doesn't mean you won't like it in college. College-level courses are quite different from high school, and you might discover a new interest in something you previously dismissed. For instance, the desire for a study abroad experience might motivate you to re-focus on learning a foreign language even if you didn't like studying foreign languages in high school. Your high school science options might have been limited to biology or chemistry or physics. But in college you have the chance to study in specialty areas such as meteorology, geology, zoology, or nutrition—all science classes that cover a broader range of subjects that might be more interesting to you.

Meta-Majors: The Netflix/Amazon Approach to Selecting a Major

You know how when you finish binging the last season of your favorite series on Netflix, Netflix immediately says, "If you enjoyed this series, you will enjoy _____" and then it gives you several ideas of similar shows that might appeal? Amazon does the same thing, "If you liked this set of earbuds, check out this other one." We can do something similar with majors.

Usually when you look at a list of majors offered by your college, you're looking at an alphabetical list. And the list can quickly become overwhelming. If you go to a large university, you might have as many as two hundred majors to choose from. That's a lot of decision-making.

But what if we group the majors into what could be called "meta-majors," larger groupings of majors that focus on a specific area of interest. It could be that if one major within a meta-major is appealing to you, others might also be appealing. Looking at majors through the lens of meta-majors can help you see new options you might not have considered. Many high schools offer one or two classes in the social sciences—psychology or government, for example. But in college, the social science meta-major will offer many more options. And if you find yourself locked out of one particular major due to grades or lacking the right prerequisites, there might be another major within that grouping that would work just as well for you.

Another advantage of looking at meta-majors is you can also think about general career fields that likely fit within those meta-majors, knowing that the career options in all are quite flexible.

So let's try an exercise that looks at meta-majors.

Meta-Major Fair Exercise

Picture this: You're going into a "majors fair" your college is offering. You see eight tables around the room, each table representing a meta-major. The professors who represent the departments are standing at their tables waiting to offer advice. Their students are there as well to give you the inside scoop on what it's like to study that major. Look over the room for a minute and without knowing anything more about the actual majors contained in the meta-major, which table would you likely wander over to first?

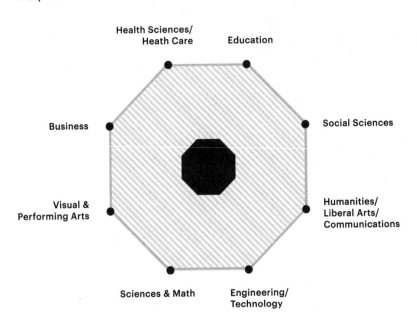

Jot down your first two choices and a quick note about why you chose them:

META-MAJOR CHOICE	WHY I THINK I WOULD LIKE THIS AREA
1	
2	

Now, given that, let's take a deeper dive into what majors you might find (depending on your school) in each of those meta-majors. We're not only going to look at the specific major within each meta-major, we're also going to look at an interesting classification for majors in general: the Holland Code.

The Holland Code was created by Dr. John Holland, who believed that work settings and personality types often overlapped. To organize his system and keep it relatively simple, he created six basic "types" of people and the places where they would likely enjoy working and fit in, so to speak. It wouldn't be a stretch to say that professors who specialize in certain fields of study would "fit" the typical characteristics of that field of study. We'll continue to apply this theory later when analyzing work settings, but for now let's apply his ideas to college majors.

The six types of people, work settings, and majors (abbreviated as RIASEC) can be broken down as follows.

- **Realistic:** Realistic people enjoy hands-on work and like seeing the results of what they build or create. They enjoy working with tools, objects, machines, and animals. They also generally like outdoor work. They tend to focus on careers that will make money or produce goods.

- **Investigative:** Investigative people are intellectually curious. They enjoy theory-based study such as the sciences and math, and they like solving problems. They like to interpret and analyze people and data. They value intellectual pursuits and focus on objective analysis.

- **Artistic:** Artistic people are creative with ideas or in creative fields such as music and art. They prefer work environments that are less structured and offer opportunities for self-expression. They like applying their imagination and intuition to their studies.

- **Social:** Social people enjoy working with others in a helping capacity. They like educating, training, or counseling people. They also are drawn to health care settings where they have the potential to heal and cure people. Serving others is an important value for social people.

- **Enterprising:** Enterprising people also enjoy working with people, but with a different focus. They are interested in influencing individuals for a business or political gain. They enjoy persuading others to purchase something or to vote in a particular way.

- **Conventional:** Conventional people prefer activities that focus on order and management. They like sorting, classifying, identifying, and organizing information or data. They tend to be particularly strong with details.

Let's apply this RIASEC model to your meta-majors and see what shows up for you. Take a look at the many majors possible within a meta-major and also note which RIASEC codes fit you. For instance, if you're interested in psychology it might be because of the "social" aspects of studying people and their behaviors. Or your interest might be more "investigative" in nature if you enjoy the research side of the major. Knowing what lies behind your interest in a subject and using the Holland code to identify that interest may help you find related majors if your primary major isn't available at your school.

As you look at the following list, circle the majors that might interest you. Keep in mind that some majors might fit into different meta-major categories depending on your college or university. For example, video game design is a major that could be listed under computer sciences, engineering, or the arts. For that reason, video game design could also fit into either artistic or investigative or even social Holland codes. So review the following majors and identify the likely Holland Code you would apply to it based on your interests:

META-MAJOR/ LIKELY HOLLAND CODE	TYPICAL MAJORS
Business E = Enterprising C = Conventional	Accounting and actuarial studies, agriculture business and management, business, business communications, data science/analytics, entrepreneurial studies, finance, hospital management, hospitality administration, human resources management, insurance, international business, management information systems, management sciences, managerial economics, marketing, real estate, sales, supply chain management, taxation
Education S = Social A = Artistic	Elementary education, family studies, human development, industrial education, language arts, library science, preschool education, secondary education, special education
Engineering/ Technology R = Realistic I = Investigative	Aerospace engineering, biomedical/biochemical engineering, chemical engineering, civil engineering, computer science, computer software, cybersecurity, electrical engineering, industrial engineering, information science, materials science, mechanical engineering, mechatronics and robotics, nuclear engineering

META-MAJOR/ LIKELY HOLLAND CODE	TYPICAL MAJORS
Health Sciences/ Health Care I = Investigative S = Social	Allied health diagnostic/intervention/treatment professions, athletic training, audiology, bioethics, dietetics, exercise science, health administration, health physics technology, kinesiology, nursing, nutrition, occupational therapy, pharmacology, pharmacy technology, physical therapy, pre-dental, pre-medical, pre-veterinary, public health, rehabilitation and therapeutic professions
Humanities/ Liberal Arts/ Communication A = Artistic S = Social I = Investigative	Advertising, ancient civilizations, area studies, classical languages, classics, communication disorders (speech pathology), communications, creative writing, English, ethnic studies, foreign languages, gender studies, historic preservation and conservation, history, journalism, language interpretation and translation, law, linguistics, literature, media studies, medieval studies, philosophy, professional writing, publishing, public relations, religion, religious studies, rhetoric and composition, technical and business writing
Sciences & Math I = Investigative R = Realistic	Agricultural science, animal science, apparel and textiles, applied mathematics, architecture, biochemistry, bioinformatics, biology, biophysics, botany, cellular biology, chemistry, data analytics, ecology, environmental design, evolutionary biology, forensic science, forestry, genetics, geology, mathematics, meteorology, microbiology, neurobiology, neurosciences, physics, physiology, plant science, statistics, zoology
Social Sciences S = Social I = Investigative A = Artistic	Anthropology, archaeology, cognitive science, criminal justice, criminology, economics, forensic psychology, geography, gerontology, government, international relations, library and information science, political science, psychology, public administration, public policy analysis, social services, social work, sociology, urban planning, urban studies, youth services
Visual & Performing Arts A = Artistic S = Social E = Enterprising	Acting, architecture, ceramics, conducting, documentary production, drama/theater arts, film/video, fine arts, graphic design, illustration, industrial design, interior design, landscape architecture, music composing and arranging, music performance, music, photography, studio arts, theater management, video game design, web design/digital media

Based on your review of this chart, fill in this Thought Organizer with your top choices for majors and/or minors as well as the likely RIASEC (Holland) code that fits your perspective on the major:

MAJOR/MINOR IDEAS	NAME OF MAJOR/MINOR	HOLLAND CODE
1		
2		
3		
4		
5		

Now that you've had a chance to look at the possible range of majors under the meta-majors you selected, let's examine your choices more carefully.

For those who have already declared a major, take some time to answer the following questions:

- Which meta-major group does your major belong to?
- Was that also your first choice when you looked at the fair?
- If your choice is the same (you picked the area that fits your current major), what do you like about it?
  - What courses are you considering taking?
  - What careers are you considering?
- If there's a discrepancy between what interested you versus what you are pursuing, take a moment to ponder that. Remember, college is the perfect time to explore and learn more about your interests.
  - Can you take some classes in the field that interests you?
  - Is it possible to add a minor (or second major) in the area of interest?
  - How would learning something in that area add to your education as well as open new career paths?
  - Do you need to consider changing majors?

For those who have not yet declared a major, consider these questions:

- Did you circle more than one major? Maybe even more than one meta-major? Hopefully you did. This will allow you to compare your choices and decide which is most interesting to you.

- Don't panic if the major(s) you selected aren't offered at your school. Consider taking a major that is closely related, and plan to do internships and independent studies that allow you to research and study your area of interest. You might be able to take a semester or two at a school that offers a major you can't get at your current school. Just work with your academic advisor and the registrar's office to make sure you can transfer the credit to that school.

A Question for Everyone to Answer

Depending on what you learned through this exercise, are you interested in combining majors or adding a minor to create an interesting career niche or specialization? For instance, what if you selected a humanities major, like "Spanish," and then added a business minor? Or a double-major in Spanish and business? Can you already see the career possibilities? Your knowledge of Spanish could fit easily into a variety of business careers and greatly enhance your resume and chances of standing out in your field.

Take a look at these possible combinations and think about how they might enhance your career options:

Foreign Language + Business =
Psychology + African American Studies =
Engineering + Creative Writing =
History + Graphic Arts =
Theatre Arts + Political Science =

So even though you don't have to let future career plans affect what you major in, you can always be thinking about how you could creatively combine majors and minors to acquire the knowledge and skills for whatever career field you are considering. Later you can think about why an employer might be particularly interested in your unique combination of majors and minors.

Making a Major Decision

At this point you know a lot about majors. But how do you decide which to pursue? By what you want to do in the future? By what you think you "need" to take in order to get into graduate or professional schools? That reasoning is fine in some cases, but here's a better focus: What do you want to learn? And why do you want to learn that body of knowledge?

Stop for a moment and think about this. Get out your notebook or a piece of paper and fill in the following Thought Organizer:

SUBJECT/MAJOR I'M CONSIDERING	WHAT I HOPE TO LEARN/STUDY	WHAT CAREERS MIGHT RELATE

By now you should have your major ideas narrowed down. If you're still unsure or questioning, keep researching and talking to professors, students, and others who will have personal knowledge of each major.

Choosing Classes Whether or Not You Have a Major

In chapter 3, we're going to look at skills you can acquire in your classes, but as you consider what courses to take, look for programs where:

- You can work on projects in teams or groups.
- You can engage in active problem-solving, in math or science or in real-world situations or issues.
- You can make public presentations.
- You can write reflective papers that help clarify your thinking about a topic.
- You can take essay exams that allow you to develop your thoughts and reasoning skills.
- There are strong expectations (and not always the easy "A").
- You will learn new information.
- Participation is expected.
- Your thoughts and ideas are appreciated.

Let's go back to that Thought Organizer you created about your possible majors on page 32, and add another column:

SUBJECT/ MAJOR I'M CONSIDERING	WHAT I HOPE TO LEARN/STUDY	WHAT CAREERS MIGHT RELATE	WHAT SKILLS/ COMPETENCIES WILL I ACQUIRE

At this point you should have some strong ideas for the major you're likely to pursue, as well as some ideas to keep investigating if you haven't decided yet. You have one more exercise to do before we leave this chapter.

A Four-Year Thought Organizer

Before we move on to identifying all the skills, knowledge, and interests you will bring to the workplace, let's look at key activities you can do during your four years in college. Don't let this framework be another source of stress for you. Most of the suggested activities can be done any time during your college career, so if you're a senior and you haven't done any of the career-related suggestions, no worries. Just start now. If your timeline through college is different, just adjust the years by what works for you.

On the following pages is a sample Thought Organizer with suggestions for what to focus on. Cross out the items as you complete them, as well as the ones that don't apply. Then write in your own ideas.

First Year

SCHOOL-RELATED ACTIVITIES	CAREER-RELATED ACTIVITIES
☐ Review the academic catalog's info about degrees and majors.	☐ Consider this an "information gathering" year.
☐ Meet with your academic advisor and discuss the plan for your first year.	☐ Check out your career center online.
☐ Double-check any advanced placement or transfer credits.	☐ Log in to whatever career center account they use so you can access job and internship listings.
☐ Start exploring majors.	☐ Fill out your profile on your career center account as completely as possible and update as needed.
☐ Visit the bookstore to explore interesting books related to specific courses or majors.	☐ Schedule an appointment with a counselor or coach or just drop in to discuss options.
☐ Take at least one interesting elective course if you can. Explore something new.	☐ Explore your interests and abilities at the career center.
☐ Notice new skills you're acquiring through classes. (See chapter 3 for more info.)	☐ Look for workshops or services for first-year or undeclared students.
☐ If considering medical school, meet with the pre-med advisor.	☐ Join student organizations.
☐ Check out offices that can help you succeed, such as tutoring services, writing centers, well-being or counseling centers, and diversity-support offices.	☐ Create a basic resume using your high school resume as a starting point.
☐ Look for major fairs or other ways to examine different majors at your school.	☐ Create a summer experience plan. (See chapter 10 for more info.)
☐ Attend your classes. Keep your grades as high as possible.	☐ Consider creating a portfolio (online or in a physical folder) of your papers, projects, or other activities.
	☐ Attend programs on resume writing or beginning the job search.
	☐ Consider micro-internships to build your resume (see chapter 10).

Sophomore Year

SCHOOL-RELATED ACTIVITIES	CAREER-RELATED ACTIVITIES
☐ Meet with your academic advisor to ensure you're taking the right courses to finish your degree on time.	☐ Start taking leadership roles in student organizations.
☐ Investigate study abroad options for next year.	☐ Start testing out possible careers by shadowing, interning, or volunteering at an organization that interests you.
☐ Begin honing in on a major you enjoy and where you want to learn more.	☐ Attend employer information sessions, as well as career workshops.
☐ Declare your major.	☐ Research potential internships, part-time work, and volunteer programs to build experience.
☐ Talk to current students to learn more.	
☐ Take another trip to the bookstore and review the textbooks for different classes and majors to clarify your interest in your major.	☐ Update your resume.
	☐ Gather information and practice your elevator pitch and interviewing skills by attending career fairs and other employer events.
☐ Thinking of grad/professional school? Begin researching your options. Note any required courses so you can fit them into your schedule.	☐ Create your LinkedIn account.
	☐ Check out alumni and parent events related to networking and careers.
☐ If your grades are strong, check in with the fellowship office to learn about opportunities such as Fulbright, Luce, Rhodes, or Marshall scholarships.	☐ Develop a summer experience plan (see chapter 10).
	☐ Attend programs about internships.

Junior Year

SCHOOL-RELATED ACTIVITIES	CAREER-RELATED ACTIVITIES
☐ Study abroad.	☐ Continue seeking leadership options with student groups.
☐ Seek out classes where you will develop more skills, such as presentations, academic research, and class projects (see chapter 3).	☐ Focus your career plans on key areas of interest. Seek out a career coach if you are still undecided.
☐ Get to know the faculty in your department and make sure they know you. Connect with faculty who might write letters of recommendation in future.	☐ Research graduate school options and admission requirements, including standardized tests.
	☐ Consider developing a portfolio of work if appropriate.

continued →

Junior Year (continued)

SCHOOL-RELATED ACTIVITIES	CAREER-RELATED ACTIVITIES
☐ Add on a minor or second major, if desired. ☐ Meet with your advisor to ensure appropriate progress toward graduation.	☐ Update your resume and target it to fields of interest. Note areas where you need to add more experience or education. ☐ Seek a summer internship or job related to your interests (see chapter 10). ☐ Keep in touch with the fellowship office if planning to apply for one. ☐ Attend programs related to your future interests.

Senior Year

SCHOOL-RELATED ACTIVITIES	CAREER-RELATED ACTIVITIES
☐ Complete final or capstone projects. ☐ Make sure you have completed all academic requirements for graduation. ☐ Talk to faculty about graduate school plans. ☐ Take classes you've always wanted to take. ☐ Continue to seek classes and experiences to build skills.	☐ Create final resumes targeted to field(s) of interest. ☐ Get resume reviewed at career center. ☐ Attend job fairs, employer information sessions, and other programs. ☐ Attend networking events. ☐ Network with alumni and parents. ☐ Update your LinkedIn account to focus on areas of interest. ☐ Apply to graduate or professional schools. Take entrance exams as needed. ☐ Use your career center's database to find potential internships and jobs. ☐ Schedule a mock interview and practice interviewing with family and friends. ☐ Sign up for job interviews related to your field of interest, even if the position isn't exactly what you are seeking. You may learn something new. ☐ Research career field thoroughly. ☐ Apply for post-graduate fellowships, if qualified.

This chapter tackled a lot of valuable information that ultimately will relate to your job search. By practicing self-compassion and paying attention to your stress level, you will approach the job search with greater resiliency and grit. Taking a thoughtful approach to choosing your major will increase the likelihood that you will find both meaning and satisfaction in your time at college and beyond. And mining your classes for the skills and knowledge you are acquiring will ensure that you can develop a great resume and potential stories for interviews and graduate school essays. You are truly setting yourself up for a much easier, efficient, and effective job search. Not to mention a safe landing in your chosen destination.

Watch Out for Weed-Out Classes

As you plan your classes, watch out for "weed out" courses that are especially designed to be difficult and "weed out" students from the major or from a career plan. For instance, it's not unusual for a chemistry or biology class to be used as a "weed out" course for students considering medical school. This is not something you'll likely hear from the school or the professor, but students will tell you, so ask. Here's why that matters: let's say you did well in biology in high school so you're thinking of taking biology for your natural science requirement. However, you learn that biology is one of the required pre-med courses, and you've heard it's especially hard. This might be a great time to take a completely different science course such as astronomy or geology, which will allow you to learn something new (and potentially interesting) as well as not compete with pre-med students. The class will still be rigorous, of course, but it's less likely to be as stressful.

Sometimes popular majors will also have weed-out sections or various requirements before you can declare their major. They might require a certain grade in an introductory class. In these cases, go for it, if you want the major. Just have a Plan B in mind if you don't attain the necessary prerequisites for the major.

Find Career Satisfaction through Your Interests and Values

———

The next two chapters start where every great job search starts: with *you*. The mistake many job seekers make is starting with the job market. They look at what's out there and guess where they might fit. But one of the strengths of the Parachute System is that it starts with you, not the job market. What fits *you*? Where will *you* be happy? In this chapter, we're going to examine two of the four key factors to consider when thinking about your future: your interests and your values. Examining these areas in detail, as well as your skills and knowledge in the next chapter, will help you develop a strong and well-rounded portrait of yourself and what you have to offer an employer.

It's important to note that these factors may or may not point you directly to a specific job. What they will do is create a pattern of ideas and possibilities that will help you find your "fit."

Your interests and values are an important part of the job-seeking process because finding work that interests you and supports your values will make you more satisfied and happier wherever you apply your skills and knowledge.

By the end of this section of the book, you will have a full Backpack ready to take into your job search. The profile you create for your Backpack will describe who you really are and who you want to be—because it isn't just about the skills, knowledge, and interests you have now, it's also about the skills, knowledge, and interests you want to develop in the future.

- What new interests have you developed since starting college?
- What are your core values and how are they changing or developing?
- Where would you like to grow your knowledge?
- What skills would you like to acquire in the future?
- Can you acquire skills through a job or will you need more schooling?

By the end of the next two chapters, you will have your answers.

Finding and Identifying Your Interests

Your interests can be an important element of your career, but that doesn't mean you need to include every interest in your career plans. In fact, it can be a good idea to keep your interests separate from a career, particularly if you enjoy them for the pleasure they bring.

Some people use the word "passion" when describing their interests. Don't be concerned if you can't identify any passions, or if your "passions" tend to be focused on your pets or important people in your life. The word "passion" can be a turnoff if you don't feel that way about your work, and it can create an undue pressure to find this perfect career that fits your "passions." If you are passionate about something, and you want to make it your career, great! Do it. But it's okay to not have passion. Focus on interests and skills instead. It's more important that you stay curious, flexible, and open to new things.

What interests do you have that could be combined creatively to make a unique career? What new interests have you developed since starting college? Are they worth considering as a possible career?

We're going to try some exercises to help you identify and analyze your interests. Relax as you work on them. Have fun—after all, you're exploring yourself and your interests. Don't try to make them fit into a job. If you like dogs, write down that you like dogs. No one will ask you to choose a career with dogs (unless you want one). If you're tempted to skip over the exercises, don't. Stop right now. Set a timer for twenty minutes and work on the exercises. When the time is up, you have a choice: you can keep writing and doing the exercises, or you can quit and try later.

Twenty Things I Like

Let's have some fun here and start with a simple exercise that can be very revealing in unexpected ways. Take out a piece of paper and number the lines up to twenty. Now, write down twenty things you like. ("Twenty things?" Yes. I know that can be hard. It's okay to list things like favorite colors, places to live, TV shows, and so on.) Stop here and make your list.

TWENTY THINGS I LIKE

Basketball
History
Law & Order SVU
Dogs
Fixing cars
Organizing projects
Using Excel
Concerts
Playing games on phone
And so on . . .

Now, look over your list. What catches your attention? Do you see anything that might apply to your future or your life? Is your list inspiring anything in you?

• • •

When writer Julia Cameron made a similar list, she discovered that many things she liked (colors, even!) applied to the Southwest. She had almost nothing on her list that applied to New York City, where she was currently living. So she moved to Santa Fe, New Mexico, and started a whole new life.

• • •

Tip: The "Twenty Things I Like" list is a great idea to try every year. Consider making it a ritual—create a list every New Year's Day or on your birthday. And save your lists. Don't look at your previous lists—just do it from scratch each year. Then compare the lists. What has changed and why?

• • •

This list is a great start to identifying your interests and what's important to you. Let's analyze your interests in a more formal way using a Thought Organizer.

Career Interest Analyzer

We're going to examine your interests in terms of what you like to read, watch or listen to, do, or learn. Fill it out with whatever comes to mind:

READ	WATCH/LISTEN	DO	LEARN
What books, websites, magazines, or blogs do you like? What topics interest you? What would you read more of if you could? Fiction or nonfiction?	What TV shows, movies, or videos do you like? What podcasts do you listen to? What music do you like?	What activities do you enjoy? Creative projects? Sports? Consider using verbs such as "organizing," "leading," "playing," "creating," and so on.	What subjects do you enjoy learning? What topics do you search on the internet? What classes have you most enjoyed?

As you look over this list, you will probably notice your interests are evolving.

- What are some of your long-term interests?
- What new interests are showing up since you started college?
- When you have these new interests, do you just make room for them or do you let old interests go?
- What are you most enjoying now?

All of your answers can be clues to not only the types of work that might interest you, but also how you can make sure your life is well-rounded and interesting.

Take a few minutes to analyze this list you created. Pretend the list belonged to someone else. What would you say about that person? What do you already know about them based on what they are interested in?

Now write a description of yourself based on this list:

_____

_____

_____

Explore Your Interests Online

There are lots of interest inventories online. Here are a few of my favorites.

- **O*NET** is a great site for uncovering career-related interests. Their interest explorer will give you all kinds of career suggestions related to your interests:
  https://www.mynextmove.org/explore/ip

- **Career Onestop** also offers a quick interest assessment that can be found here:
  https://www.careeronestop.org/toolkit/careers/interest-assessment.aspx

- **The Minnesota Office of Higher Education** offers an interest assessment designed for college students:
  https://www.ohe.state.mn.us/sPages/interestAssessment.cfm

- **The University of Missouri's Career Center** publishes a similar exercise for discovering your interests and possible careers. Check out the Career Interests Game for a complete profile related to your RIASEC code:
  https://www.career.missouri.edu/career-interest-game

•••

Olivia's list showed that she likes singer-songwriter music. She likes songs that have interesting lyrics that tell stories. She also likes to read memoirs and biographies. She likes to read about celebrities because their lives are usually quite complicated and she enjoys learning how they recovered from whatever problem they were having. Her favorite classes so far have been literature classes. As a child, she read every Harry Potter book and The Chronicles of Narnia. She likes to watch detective and mystery shows on TV and is particularly fond of some of the British mysteries. She worked at a camp one summer and her favorite part of the day was telling stories around the campfire in the evening. She also grew up with two dogs and she knows she'll always find a way to have a dog in her life. •••

What we can see here is a pattern: people, stories, caring about others, uncovering and solving mysteries, and so on. She seems to be a "people-person" who enjoys diving into a subject rather than settling for simple amusement. Because she enjoys storytelling, she might want to look at a major where she can study people and their stories: perhaps a social science, like anthropology or psychology, or an English or history major where she could study the lives of others. As she starts to pursue this direction, she will hone her likes and dislikes and that may ultimately lead her to a career path. But we're not there yet. So let's keep going.

Campus Activities Exercise

Remember the Meta-Major Fair Exercise you did on page 26? (You didn't do it? That's okay, just play along here.) Let's apply the same concept to interests, except this time you're at a college activities fair. It's your chance to talk to like-minded students who are interested in the same things you're interested in. You get to choose the activities, clubs, or groups you'd like to be involved in. Look around the "room" on page 44 and select the table you'd go to first. What activities would you select from that table? (Feel free to add more to reflect what you're already involved in.) After that first table, which table would you go to next? And then which would be your third choice in tables?

Notice that some of the same activities are at different tables. That's because you might explore different parts of an activity. For instance, you could choose to be on the school newspaper because you like to write (Table "A"), because you like investigative reporting (Table "I"), or because you want to write editorials and influence others (Table "E"). It's okay to list whatever table you'd like for an activity based on how you see yourself involved in that area.

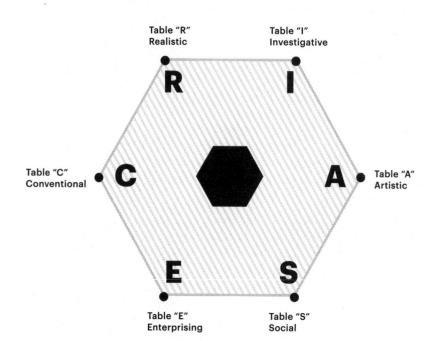

Table "R"
Realistic

Table "I"
Investigative

Table "C"
Conventional

Table "A"
Artistic

Table "E"
Enterprising

Table "S"
Social

TABLES	ACTIVITIES/CLUBS/ORGANIZATIONS		
Table "R" Realistic: This table features clubs or organizations that focus on athletics, computers, ROTC, and other "hands-on" activities.	• athletic teams • bowling • building models • climbing walls • coding • computer user groups	• digital gaming • drones • exercise classes • golf • horseback riding • hunting/fishing • kayaking	• landscaping or gardening • repairing cars • robotics • ROTC • target shooting • woodworking
Table "I" Investigative: This table features clubs or organizations that focus on science, gaming, health, computers, or research-related activities.	• astronomy • board games • chemical society • chess • crossword puzzles • math	• modeling • nanotechnology • pre-med society • school newspaper • science fiction • sports analytics	• Sudoku • video games • virtual reality • visiting museums

Table "A" Artistic: This table features clubs or organizations that focus on creative endeavors.	• art organizations • bands • Bollywood dancing • choir • college radio • concerts • dance organizations • designing sets • desktop publishing	• drama groups • film society • glee club • homemade crafts • improv comedy • music jams • orchestra • painting • performing • photography	• playing an instrument • poetry slam • scrapbooking • sewing • student theatre group • travel • visiting art galleries • writing
Table "S" Social: This table features clubs or organizations that focus on connecting with people in a variety of ways.	• attending sporting events • campus fundraisers • caring for children • discussion groups • diversity-related organizations • environmental organizations	• habitat for humanity • helping others with personal concerns • language and culture club • parties • political organizations • racial and social justice organizations	• refugee assistance groups • religious activities • service fraternities • tutoring organizations • volunteering • writing letters
Table "E" Enterprising: This table features clubs or organizations that focus on activities related to professions, businesses, entrepreneurial activities, or politics.	• business-related organizations • debate clubs • entrepreneurial clubs • investment clubs • leading campus or community organizations	• mock trial competitions • national model united nations • political clubs • political discussions • pre-law society	• profession-based clubs • public speaking • selling or fundraising • student government
Table "C" Conventional: This table features clubs or organizations that focus on organizational structure and activities such as collecting or record-keeping.	• accounting-related organizations • bookkeeping activities • card and board games • collecting items (rocks, stamps, coins . . .)	• collecting memorabilia • collectors' clubs • computer coding • economics club • genealogy • investment club • maintaining club records and files	• organizing events • parliamentarian or meeting rules manager • ROTC • treasurer role in organization • writing family histories

What letters correspond with the tables you selected? Put them here:

——— ——— ———

If you completed the meta-majors exercise in chapter 1:

- How close were your letters to the ones you selected previously?
- What differences did you discover?
- How consistent are you in your patterns of interest?

You are gathering potentially powerful tools for your upcoming job and internship searches.

Now review all the information you've collected about your interests. Which interests really pop for you? Which ones would you like to keep exploring for possible career connections?

List your top three to five potential career-related interests:

1 _____

2 _____

3 _____

4 _____

5 _____

Identifying What's Important: Your Values

One of the most essential parts of determining whether you will enjoy your work is whether your work fits with your values: what is most important to you. Knowing your values can be as important as knowing your skills. If you find a work setting that uses your skills, but doesn't fit your values, you may succeed, but you will likely not be happy or feel like you fit in.

For instance, let's say one of your strong skills is accounting or budgeting. So you start looking for jobs that will allow you to work in the financial area for an organization. But one of your values is protecting the earth. You're probably not going to be happy as an accountant for a company that you know is polluting the rivers. You would probably rather work for a company that shares your values about the environment. This could mean you work for an environmental firm or maybe a company that focuses on wind or solar power, or for a lobbying organization. There are many, many places that will fit your values: it's just important to know what they are. Sometimes you'll figure out your values if you work at a place that doesn't fit you. By observing what you don't like about an organization, you can often discover values you didn't know you had.

• • •

Throughout life, Taylor (pronouns they/them) had always been an excellent student. They took a values assessment and discovered their top values were learning, helping others, and being creative. They loved the classroom environment, and they spent a lot of time tutoring in high school. They thought it was a no-brainer to start their first year as a major in education with plans to pursue a career in elementary education. Taylor was pursuing an elementary education degree when they saw a poster on a bulletin board asking for volunteers at a speech pathology clinic. They thought the experience would look good on their resume, so they applied. The more they volunteered, the more the agency let them do, and the agency even invited them to do an internship for credit. They learned how much they enjoyed working with their young patients and the patients' parents in a very different setting. Rather than teach in a traditional classroom, they realized they could teach the children and parents how to use this new technology to hear better. Taylor discovered that part of the reason they liked the school setting was they really hadn't explored other ideas, and Taylor

Exploring Values Online

———

Would you like to take a free online test that will help you identify important values? The Values in Action survey is an excellent resource. You can access it at either of these sites.

Values in Action survey:
https://www.authentichappiness.sas.upenn.edu

VIA Institute on Character:
https://www.viacharacter.org/character-strengths

now knows they like medical settings, too. They switched their major to speech pathology and audiology and plans a different career that will align with their values.

• • •

Are you wondering what your values might be? Here are some exercises to help you figure that out.

Values Exercise

Take a look at the following list of values. Check the ones that you think apply to you. Circle your top five values.

Achievement	Adventure	Artistic Expression	Authenticity
Autonomy	Balance	Beauty	Challenge
Collaboration	Compassion	Competition	Contribution
Creativity	Curiosity	Fame	Fun
Happiness	Helping Others	Helping Society	Independence
Influence	Justice	Leadership	Leisure
Prestige	Recognition	Relationships	Responsibility
Social Justice	Spirituality/Religion	Success	Support
Trustworthiness	Variety	Wealth	Wisdom

Now that you've identified five values, write a few sentences about each one. What experiences have you had that illustrate those values? If you say you value "helping society" for example, when have you had a chance to do that? Or, what do you hope to do in the future that will illustrate your desire to help society?

Value #1: _____

_____

Value #2: _____

_____

Value #3: _____

_____

Value #4: _____

_____

Value #5: _____

Now that you have more closely examined these values, which ones do you feel are the strongest or most important to you?

Were you stuck on ways to demonstrate how your values apply in your life? Interestingly there's a lot of overlap between interests and values. Knowing what's important about your interests can say a lot about your personality, style, and values. Let's look at how your interests might reflect your values. Go back to those interests you identified on page 46.

- Write a short sentence or two about what you particularly like about that interest area.
- Ask yourself what that interest means to you.
- Why do you do it?
- What's fun about it?
- What's most important to you about it?

Here are some sample student comments about their interests in sports. In each case, the students said they liked certain sports or physical activities. Some watched them on TV, some liked to read about them as well, but none of the students was talented enough to play them professionally. Notice how different they are and how they reflect important values for each student.

• • •

"I play basketball to relax. The game is so crazy fast and busy that it stops all my thinking about my problems or what else is happening in my life. When I'm on the court, I am in my zone." (Possible values: balance, fun.)

"I play golf because I like the simple outcome: a score. I know that much of that score is under my control. A simple adjustment in my wrist movement can result in a better score. I can set internal goals to improve parts of my game: long, short, or putting. I can play alone and try to improve, or I can play with others for the competition. But ultimately I like setting goals that only I can achieve. (Possible values: autonomy, challenge, competition.)

"I dance because I have to. Every time I'm on that dance floor, I'm me. I'm expressing something I'm feeling. I am unlimited: I can move in any direction I want. Sometimes I feel like I could fly. I can always learn something new: a new step, a better warm-up. I get to create my space

any way I want just by how I choose to move." (Possible values: artistic expression, beauty, creativity.)

"I play video games because I love the competition and the constant striving to go to the next level. I also like interacting with my online friends—many of whom I don't know outside the game. And yet we have this common bond of the game and we help each other by providing tips and sharing rewards. Gaming seems solitary to someone watching it, but it's not: it's very social and I have even made new friends locally through my gaming connections." (Possible values: challenge, competition, collaboration, fun.)

"I am in a hiking club and once a month we volunteer to do a trash pickup on our hikes. I have been doing it for about a year now. We clean up the trails as well as the land near them. I like using my hikes to do something positive for others and for the environment. My hikes always help me cope with stress, and if I've had a bad week and don't feel good about myself or life, I think about how my work each month makes life better for others. And I like knowing I'm hiking with people who care. That's important." (Possible values: compassion, contribution, helping society.)

• • •

If you haven't already, take a few minutes and write a few statements about why you pursue your interests. Then look at the list of values and see which ones your interests might reflect.

Purpose Exercise

For a final exercise in this chapter, let's expand the concept of values to "life purpose." You're young and likely still figuring out what is most meaningful to you, but try this exercise called "The Purpose for My Life" that Richard Bolles created. You might find it inspires you to move in a whole new direction. Look at the diagram on the opposite page.

Which of the spheres or purposes appeal to you? Take your time to ponder. Try circling the elements that are most important to you.

- One way to think about this is to finish the sentence, "I want there to be more _____." What does the world need more of, in your opinion?
- Which of the spheres highlights that?
- What area would you most like to contribute to?
- Where could you help to improve one of the spheres?
- How would you change/alter the spheres?
- What could you do that would make a difference? What would you like to do?

The Purpose for My Life:

I Want There to Be More . . .

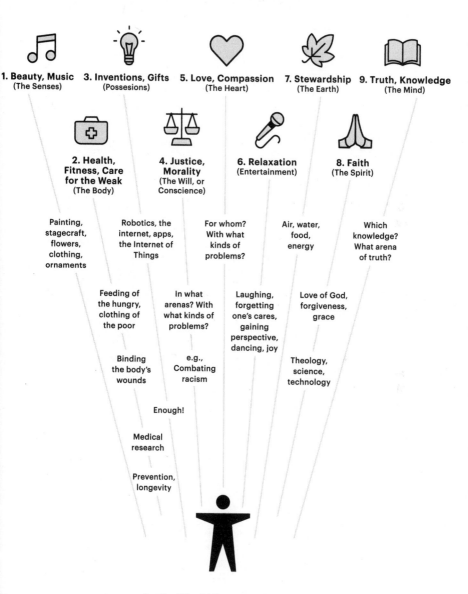

1. Beauty, Music
(The Senses)

3. Inventions, Gifts
(Possesions)

5. Love, Compassion
(The Heart)

7. Stewardship
(The Earth)

9. Truth, Knowledge
(The Mind)

2. Health,
Fitness, Care
for the Weak
(The Body)

4. Justice,
Morality
(The Will, or
Conscience)

6. Relaxation
(Entertainment)

8. Faith
(The Spirit)

Painting,
stagecraft,
flowers,
clothing,
ornaments

Robotics, the
internet, apps,
the Internet of
Things

For whom?
With what
kinds of
problems?

Air, water,
food,
energy

Which
knowledge?
What arena
of truth?

Feeding of
the hungry,
clothing of
the poor

In what
arenas? With
what kinds of
problems?

Laughing,
forgetting
one's cares,
gaining
perspective,
dancing, joy

Love of God,
forgiveness,
grace

Binding
the body's
wounds

e.g.,
Combating
racism

Theology,
science,
technology

Enough!

Medical
research

Prevention,
longevity

. . . in the World Because I Was Here

You might enjoy reading how Richard Bolles described your possible work in the different spheres. See if anything he says makes you rethink how your values and interests might relate to your future plans.

The Sphere of the Senses

The question is: *When you have finished your life here on Earth, do you want there to be more beauty in the world, because you were here? If so, what kind of beauty entrances you? Is it art, music, flowers, photography, painting, staging, crafts, clothing, jewelry, or what?* If this is your main purpose in life, then write one paragraph about it.

The Sphere of the Body

The question is: *When you have finished your life here on Earth, do you want there to be more wholeness, fitness, or health in the world; more healing of the body's wounds; more feeding of the hungry, and clothing of the poor, because you were here? Which issue in particular?* If this is your main purpose in life, then write one paragraph about it.

The Sphere of Possessions

The question is: *Is your major concern the often false love of possessions in this world? When you have finished your life here on Earth, do you want there to be better stewardship of what we possess—as individuals, as a community, as a nation—in the world, because you were here? Do you want to see simplicity, quality (rather than quantity), and a broader emphasis on the word "enough," rather than on the words "more, more"? If so, in what areas of human life in particular?* If this is your main purpose in life, then write one paragraph about it.

The Sphere of the Will or Conscience

The question is: *When you have finished your life here on Earth, do you want there to be more morality, more justice, more righteousness, more honesty in the world, because you were here? In what areas of human life or history, in particular? And in what geographical area?* If this is your main purpose in life, then write one paragraph about it.

The Sphere of the Heart

The question is: *When you have finished your life here on Earth, do you want there to be more love and compassion in the world, because you were here? Love or compassion for whom? Or for what?* If this is your main purpose in life, then write one paragraph about it.

The Sphere of Entertainment
The question is: *When you have finished your life here on Earth, do you want there to be more lightening of people's loads, more giving them perspective, more helping them to forget their cares for a spell; do you want there to be more laughter in the world, and joy, because you were here? If so, what particular kind of entertainment do you want to contribute to the world?* If this is your main purpose in life, then write one paragraph about it.

The Sphere of the Earth
The question is: *Is the planet on which we stand, your major concern? When you have finished your life here on Earth, do you want there to be better protection of this fragile planet, more exploration of the world or the universe—exploration, not exploitation—more dealing with its problems and its energy, because you were here? If so, which problems or challenges, in particular, draw your heart and soul?* If this is your main purpose in life, then write one paragraph about it.

The Sphere of the Spirit
The question is: *When you have finished your life here on Earth, do you want there to be more spirituality in the world, more faith, more compassion, more forgiveness, more love for a higher power and the human family in all its diversity, because you were here? If so, with what ages, people, or with what parts of human life?* If this is your main purpose in life, then write one paragraph about it.

The Sphere of the Mind
The question is: *When you have finished your life here on Earth, do you want there to be more knowledge, truth, or clarity in the world, because you were here? Knowledge, truth, or clarity concerning what in particular?* If this is your main purpose in life, then write one paragraph about it.

At this point you should have a pretty good idea of your key interests and values. At least for now. Remember, you are always learning and developing new interests and uncovering your values.

So consider this a start. And an excellent one at that.

To finish out this chapter and start packing your Backpack, write down the top three to five interests you might want to take into the workplace:

1 _____

2 _____

3 _____

4 _____

5 _____

And now jot down the top three to five values that are important to you in whatever career you ultimately pursue:

1 _____

2 _____

3 _____

4 _____

5 _____

CHAPTER 3

Find Career Success through Your Skills and Knowledge

In this chapter we're going to delve into what are arguably the most important elements you have to offer a potential employer: your skills and your knowledge. Skills and knowledge are interrelated, of course, but not the same thing. It's one thing to know something, but can you demonstrate that you can use that knowledge in the appropriate way? There's a big difference between reading about how to ski and actually skiing. Until you take your knowledge for a test drive, it's just information. This chapter will help you identify your knowledge and demonstrate that you have converted it into skills.

One constant I have seen in my career is that college students often are either unaware of the skills they have acquired or tend to feel they don't have any skills—other than being a student.

It's one of the reasons graduate school can be so alluring—after all, you know how to be a student. You've been a student for more than twelve years now, so what's a few more years? Before you even think about graduate or professional school (and there's a lot more information about that in chapter 11), let's stop and learn more about the skills and knowledge you already have. You may find that further study isn't needed.

Having the correct skills and knowledge will make you highly desired by employers. It is not an understatement to say that your skills will get you your job.

If you look at other career books, you will find lots of different types of skills. Skills, as defined for this system, encompass several things.

- **Job skills:** skills that are specific to the work you plan to do, such as analyzing data.
- **Transferable skills:** skills that can be used and applied in several settings.
- **Technical skills:** skills related to computers, software, or machinery.
- **Interpersonal skills:** skills that produce good relationships.
- **Soft skills:** skills that relate to your work style, such as dependability or reliability.
- **Self-management skills:** skills that focus on your behavior, such as stress management.

Many career books try to differentiate these skills, but we're not going to nitpick about this. We're going to call them all *skills*. And they are all important. The type of job you are seeking will determine the job skills you will need, but you will have a greater chance for success if you also possess the soft skills that employers are also seeking.

Another word that gets mixed into this area is "talents." How do we differentiate "talent" from "skill"? It's fairly easy: talent refers to a gift—a natural ability that can't be learned. Skill is ability we can learn but doesn't necessarily come naturally. We can be taught a skill; no one can teach talent.

You have many more skills than you realize, and the cool thing about skills is no matter where you are, you can always build more. You are never too old (or too young) to learn a new skill. You might have limitations that make it hard for you see them, or you might have to apply them differently, but you have your own unique gifts and skills that an employer will want. To make full use of your skills, you must:

- Know your skills and how to enhance or improve them
- Discover which skills you need to build and then build them
- Explain (articulate) why your skills are valuable to an employer
- Provide evidence of their existence

One way to start thinking about your skills is to consider the skills you have related to things, people, and information. Take a look at this sample list and then list your skills that fall into the following categories.

THINGS	PEOPLE	INFORMATION
Animals	Advising	Analyzing
Art materials	Assessing	Computing
Cameras	Coaching	Creating
Cars	Communicating	Drawing
Computers	Connecting	Interviewing
Food	Guiding	Inventing
Microscopes	Helping	Keeping good records
Musical instruments	Managing	Organizing
Plants	Teaching	Problem-solving
Tools	Tutoring	Researching

Career Readiness and Competencies

You might wonder why skills are so important for career success. A popular term these days is "career readiness." And the word most often applied to career readiness is "competencies." Competencies are very much like skills and knowledge. Like the word implies, you need to be competent in certain areas to succeed on your job. A lot of research has gone into identifying the most important competencies for college students. Some research relies on employer surveys; some research focuses on what professors or universities believe are important. The Pedagogy for Employability Group, the National Association of Colleges and Employers, and the College of Liberal Arts at the University of Minnesota are just a few of the organizations that have attempted to identify the most important competencies for college students.

Based on a variety of surveys, following are twenty-two key competencies that many employers are seeking. Note that not every employer is seeking every competency for a particular job. But you can expect to receive some questions during an interview related to the competencies most needed in the position you are seeking.

- Look at the chart on page 58 and place a check in the first column if you believe that competency will be needed in the job you're seeking.

- Then look to the right of the competency and place a checkmark that best describes your current level of skill in each competency area.

  - "Strong" means that you have used the competency in a variety of settings and are quite comfortable talking about it during an interview.

- "Average" means you have used the competency in one setting and are still in a learning mode. You don't have a particularly strong story about using the competency.

- "Not yet" means you have not had the opportunity to develop or use the competency. In some cases, this won't matter as the competency may not be relevant to the position you're seeking, but if you think it might be, it would be good to find a way to develop it.

WILL NEED	COMPETENCY	STRONG	AVERAGE	NOT YET
	Ability to manage others			
	Ability to work under pressure			
	Adaptability/flexibility			
	Attention to details			
	Career management			
	Critical thinking and problem-solving			
	Entrepreneurship			
	Ethical reasoning and decision-making			
	Global/intercultural fluency			
	Imagination/creativity			
	Independent working/autonomy			
	Information technology application			
	Leadership			
	Numeracy/data skills			
	Oral/written communication			
	Organizing ability			
	Professionalism and work ethic			
	Resiliency			
	Self-management/personal wellness			
	Teamwork/collaboration			
	Time management			
	Willingness to learn			

Of the competencies you listed as "strong," describe what you think that competency means.

- When and where did you demonstrate this?
- How did you develop the competency?
- What's the best example of a time when you demonstrated or used that competency?

Of the competencies you listed as "average" or "not yet":

- Which ones would you like to develop or think would be good to develop?
- What's your plan for developing them?
- Are there classes you could take, online learning such as YouTube or Udemy, or a part-time job or internship where you could develop them?

Remember the competencies that you haven't developed yet have potential for a great interview story: "I realized that to succeed in this job I would need to develop my oral communication skills. So I took a rhetoric class that required me to prepare an argument or short speech each week. Then I signed up for debate club, which really honed my speaking skills."

Here's a final interest note about competencies. When surveying employers about competencies, the National Association of Colleges and Employers (NACE) uncovered a disturbing response. Employers tend to rate students lower on competencies than the students do. For instance, one NACE survey found a particularly large gap in the area of professionalism and work ethic. The study found that "about 90 percent of students rated themselves proficient; less than half of the employers agreed."[5]

That's a huge discrepancy between what students think versus what employers observe.

Why does this matter? Well, knowing that employers don't necessarily trust your rating of your competencies, you should demonstrate your competencies through specific work examples or provide work samples (such as a paper to demonstrate your writing skills). This will make it more likely that the employer will trust your statements.

Remember, you don't need to be strong in all of the competencies but the more you can develop and be able to tell a story about how you demonstrated them, the stronger your profile will be for a potential employer.

Uncovering Your Stories: Two Exercises

I know. I know. You are already busy. You are constantly writing papers for your classes, and now you're being asked to write even more. But the two exercises here are amazingly powerful in your job search. First, they will help you uncover new knowledge about yourself and your skills. What you learn might even lead you in a whole new direction. And, you can repurpose these stories for interviews, graduate school essays, and even cover letters. So grab a cup of coffee and have fun writing about these life stories.

Exercise One: Seven Stories from Your Life

Richard Bolles developed a groundbreaking way to uncover hidden skills: write stories about them. Well, not specifically stories about your skills, but stories that will reveal your skills. In this exercise, he recommends you write seven short stories (about a page maximum) describing an interesting event in your life. If you don't have time to write a whole page, that's okay. Just write a quick paragraph explaining the situation, how you solved it, and what skills you used.

Some ideas for these stories include:

- You at your best. Think of a situation where you were at your best. What were you doing?
- A unique situation you were involved in.
- An experience where you felt alive and involved.
- A particularly rewarding experience. What made it rewarding for you?

Now take a look at the story. If you haven't already included this, add:

- Your goal. What did you want to accomplish?
- Some kind of hurdle or obstacle and how you overcame it.
- A description of what you did, step-by-step.
- A description of the outcome—preferably a measurable outcome.

The stories don't have to be grandiose, such as how you saved someone's life. (Although if you did, definitely write that story!) It's okay to pick small things or small victories in your life. Maybe it was the summer you learned to ride a horse. Or the time you offered to babysit the most difficult child in the neighborhood. And you survived. Or you organized your grandmother's finances when she started to forget to pay her bills. Maybe you taught your grandfather how to use social media to connect with his friends. There are lots of potential stories of your skills and strengths if you just start thinking about them. In fact, try brainstorming a quick list here and then decide which ones you'd like to develop further:

MY LIST OF POSSIBLE STORIES
1
2
3
4
5
6
7

Richard Bolles developed a great system to help you analyze your stories. The Parachute Skills Grid he created (pages 62 to 64) can help you quickly find the skills in your stories. Try running each of your stories through the skills lists and see what shows up. You just might find strengths you didn't realize you had.

The Parachute Skills Grid

Your Seven Stories

In the space to the left, write above each number, in turn, the name you give to each story. Begin with Story #1. Then go down the list and mark the box if you used that skill in that story.

1	2	3	4	5	6	7	SKILLS WITH PEOPLE; AS MY STORY SHOWS, I CAN . . .
							Initiate, lead, be a pioneer
							Supervise, manage
							Follow through, get things done
							Motivate
							Persuade, sell, recruit
							Consult
							Advise
							Coordinate
							Negotiate, resolve conflicts
							Help people link up or connect
							Heal, cure
							Assess, evaluate, treat
							Convey warmth and empathy
							Interview, draw out
							Raise people's self-esteem
							Instruct
							Teach, tutor, or train (individuals, groups, animals)
							Speak
							Listen
							Counsel, guide, mentor
							Communicate well, in person

1	2	3	4	5	6	7	SKILLS WITH PEOPLE; AS MY STORY SHOWS, I CAN . . . (CONTINUED)
							Communicate well, in writing
							Divert, amuse, entertain, perform, act
							Play an instrument
							Interpret, speak, or read a foreign language
							Serve, care for, follow instructions faithfully

1	2	3	4	5	6	7	SKILLS WITH DATA AND IDEAS; AS MY STORY SHOWS, I CAN . . .
							Use my intuition
							Create, innovate, invent
							Design, use artistic abilities, be original
							Visualize, including in three dimensions
							Imagine
							Use my brain
							Synthesize, combine parts into a whole
							Systematize, prioritize
							Organize, classify
							Perceive patterns
							Analyze, break down into parts
							Work with numbers, compute
							Remember people, or data, to unusual degree
							Develop, improve
							Solve problems

continued →

The Parachute Skills Grid (continued)

1	2	3	4	5	6	7	SKILLS WITH DATA AND IDEAS; AS MY STORY SHOWS, I CAN . . . (CONTINUED)
							Plan
							Program
							Research
							Examine, inspect, compare, see similarities and differences
							Use acute senses (hearing, smell, taste, sight)
							Study, observe
							Compile, keep records, file, retrieve
							Copy
1	**2**	**3**	**4**	**5**	**6**	**7**	**SKILLS WITH THINGS; AS MY STORY SHOWS, I CAN . . .**
							Control, expedite things
							Make, produce, manufacture
							Repair
							Finish, restore, preserve
							Construct
							Shape, model, sculpt
							Cut, carve, chisel
							Set up, assemble
							Handle, tend, feed
							Operate, drive
							Manipulate
							Use my body, hands, fingers, with unusual dexterity or strength

Making the Most of On-Campus Employment

——

Have you been a student worker sometime during your college years? If not, consider finding an on-campus job. Often students fail to recognize the benefits of on-campus employment. On-campus jobs often provide opportunities to take on quasi-professional roles. Many student-affairs offices, for instance, hire student workers to help with everything from staffing the front desk to running peer-programs and workshops. If you've had the opportunity to do something like this, try using the questions below to expand how you might talk about your experience and/or use the experience in a resume, cover letter, or application to graduate school.

Describe your student worker experience generally.

1   What was your title and what were your main duties or responsibilities?

2   What skills did you develop or strengthen through your experience?

3   Describe your best day in your role as a _____. What was the situation? How did you handle it? What was the outcome? How did you feel afterward?

4   What was your most challenging person or situation? How did you handle it? What was the outcome?

5   What three words would your supervisor use to describe you?

6   What three words would your students, clients, or customers use to describe you?

7   What skills or personality traits or knowledge were needed to be successful in your role?

How could you shape this story into a line or two in your cover letter, on your resume, or as part of an essay for graduate school?

Now, how could you shape this student work experience into an interesting interview story to a potential employer? Use a story from this experience to answer these potential employer questions:

- Tell me about yourself.
- Why should we hire you?
- Tell me about a time when you had to solve a problem.
- What aspect of this experience has prepared you for this job?

Exercise Two: Identifying Skills/Competencies Acquired through Your Classes

Not every class will provide you with a unique set of skills (maybe staying awake?) but think through the classes you've taken so far.

- If you wrote papers, how much research or work went into writing them?
- Was your professor a hard grader who forced you to work even harder on a particular class?
- Did you complete any other project in this course?
- What about your exams? Were they cumulative, covering an entire semester's worth of knowledge?
- Did you take a class where other students already had a background and you didn't? How did you catch up? How did you keep up?
- Did you take a course that caused you to think about a subject from a different perspective?
- Did a course teach you empathy for another culture or the experiences of someone different from you?
- Did you complete a group assignment where you had to work together with other students to complete a project and presentation?
- What was your most challenging class?

Keep in mind that very few professors will take the time to tell you what skills you are developing; you will need to figure that out. Here's a list of the skills you probably acquired in your classes whether you know it or not. Take a look at this list and start thinking about which classes you took (or plan to take) that will teach these skills.

Accountability	Adaptive thinking	Analytical thinking
Collaboration	Creativity	Critical thinking
Curiosity	Diligence	Empathy
Essay writing	Flexibility	Foreign language
Independent learning	Independent projects	Information management
Leadership	Mathematical/ data analysis	Note-taking
Patience	Perspective	Presentations
Problem-solving	Project management	Reading critically
Reflection	Researching	Scientific instrumentation
Self-discipline	Self-management	Self-motivation
Software skills	Synthesizing information	Technical skills
Time management	Understanding	Writing

Skills and Competencies from the Classes You've Taken

Try creating a chart of the skills or competencies you have acquired in your various classes throughout your time in school. If you're just starting out, you can create this list from the beginning. But even if you're a senior, try going back into the past and fill in what you remember. To refresh your memory about classes, look at your transcript or on your computer at the various papers and projects you've done over the past few years. On page 68 is a chart to complete as you take your classes. Read the sample chart first to get an idea of how you can complete yours. Create one on your computer, or just draw it on a page in your notebook.

First-year classes	Skills acquired
Introduction to Chemistry	• Scientific method: conducted basic experiments
	• Laboratory skills: managing supplies in a safe manner
	• Methodology: followed procedures
	• Patience: had to redo numerous experiments
	• Memorization and knowledge: preparation for exams
	• Self-discipline: set up own schedule for labs
	• Received a B in a course that's intended for pre-med students

Sophomore-year classes	Skills acquired
American Studies Class	• Interviewing: Interviewed a local advocate for the homeless and individuals at homeless shelter
	• Analysis: Analyzed the local homelessness situation
	• Developed compassion and empathy toward others by volunteering at shelter for two weekends

Junior-year classes	Skills acquired
Participated in special semester program in Washington, D.C., involving coursework in policy studies and a twenty-hour-per-week internship on Capitol Hill.	• Writing: Wrote twenty-page paper analyzing government policies related to homelessness
	• Understanding of political process: Acquired first-hand experience through credit-based internship on Capitol Hill
	• Networking: Networked with public policymakers and consultants and built up connections for future employment

Senior-year classes	Skills acquired
Finished requirements for major and for graduation. Took elective courses in psychology and sociology.	• Writing/research: Assisted professor with research on journal article
	• Built knowledge: Broadened my understanding of homelessness by examining the psychological and sociological elements of homelessness
	• Interviewing: Interviewed workers at a homeless shelter
	• Goal-setting/coaching: Worked with one homeless individual throughout the semester, helping him set goals for his future
	• Writing: Wrote a report for psychology class analyzing individual situation in the larger context of homelessness

Now it's your turn. Fill in this chart with the key classes you have taken. Update the chart as you progress through your college program. Remember: it's best to fill this out each semester. It's easy to forget what you've done.

First-year classes	Skills acquired
Sophomore-year classes	Skills acquired
Junior-year classes	Skills acquired
Senior-year classes	Skills acquired

How to Start Building Your Skills and Competencies

Building up your expertise and knowledge involves several steps:

1 **Paying attention.** You can't build what you're not aware of. Note your current skills.

2 **Identifying the expertise you want to build.** Know what you're lacking.

3 **Taking advantage of your time and the school calendar.** Use your summers and breaks to build skills.

4 **Seeking out new opportunities.** Look for ways to build your skills in classes, by volunteering, and so on.

5 **Building on opportunities that already exist.** If you already have an internship or job, ask for more duties that will build new skills.

6 **Noting unexpected or bonus expertise you acquired.** Maybe you were hired to do one job, but ended up doing extra activities. What skills did you learn?

7 **Recording your activities so that you can share them in the future.** It's always a good idea to write down your experiences so you don't forget.

8 **What is your plan for building new skills?**

Knowledge Section

You've been acquiring knowledge your whole life, both inside the classroom and out. Richard Bolles developed a list of ten quick ways to uncover your knowledge. Sometimes your knowledge is based on your interests, so you might find some overlap between the two. Try filling out this chart to identify some of your key areas of knowledge.

TEN QUESTIONS ABOUT KNOWLEDGE	MY ANSWER
1 What are your favorite hobbies?	
2 What do you love to talk about? What subjects could you go on about forever?	
3 What magazine articles or blogs do you like to read? What podcasts do you listen to?	
4 What current events do you follow? What newspapers do you read?	
5 What section of the bookstore do you head to?	
6 What sites on the internet do you follow?	
7 What television shows do you watch?	
8 What courses interest you the most?	
9 If you could write a book (not about your life) what would it focus on?	
10 When have you ever been so engrossed in a task you totally lost track of time? What were you doing?	

Based on the interests and information you uncovered through these questions, what are some key areas of knowledge you possess?

Still thinking about your knowledge? Here's another chart that Richard Bolles created to help you identify areas of knowledge you have acquired. He described it as a "fisherman's net": a way to capture as many ideas as you can about what you know.

Knowledge Inventory

WHAT HAVE YOU LEARNED THROUGH JOBS? THIS COULD INCLUDE SPECIFIC SKILLS, LIKE OPERATING MACHINERY OR TRAINING SOMEONE.	WHAT FIELDS OR CAREERS INTEREST YOU JUST BECAUSE? WHAT CAREER FIELDS HAVE YOU CONSIDERED OVER THE YEARS, BASED ON YOUR KNOWLEDGE?
WHAT HAVE YOU LEARNED IN SCHOOL OR OTHER TRAINING PROGRAMS?	ANY OTHER HUNCHES, BRIGHT IDEAS, OR SUBJECTS IN SCHOOL THAT YOU ENJOYED?

As you look over all the lists of the knowledge that you have acquired, it's time to sort it. There's no point in focusing on an area where you're knowledgeable but have no interest in pursuing a career related to it. Here's a quick way to sort everything. The top boxes are likely choices for future consideration as a career path. The lower boxes indicate areas where you will likely be less satisfied in related work.

I know a lot about this and I love using it:	I don't know a lot about this but would love to learn more and use it:
I know a lot about this but don't like using it:	I know relatively little about this and would prefer not to use it or learn more:

Finally, one way to powerfully enhance your knowledge is to focus not only on what you know, but what you don't know, and how you can learn it. Perhaps when you were identifying some of your knowledge areas, you realized that it would be helpful to know more about a subject. For instance, you might have indicated specific knowledge you have of a programming language, but you might also know that there's another language that would be worth learning. So use the chart below to identify what you'd like to learn, and the most efficient way you can learn it. Keep this chart around, because when you ultimately decide on your career or graduate school plans, you may find that you have more to learn. You can revise this chart then as needed.

WHAT I KNOW	WHAT I WANT TO LEARN	WHO CAN HELP?	HOW CAN I SET IT UP?

So now you can fill your Backpack with knowledge that will possibly relate to your future plans.

So much of career success is dependent on your skills and knowledge. The more you are able to demonstrate your competencies in a variety of areas, the more employable you are. Employers will overlook your major, your GPA, and even a lack of direct experience if you are able to demonstrate that you have the knowledge and skills to perform successfully on the job. Make it a plan to stay constantly aware of the new skills and knowledge you are acquiring throughout your time in college. The upcoming chapters will help you articulate the value of your skills in a way that will have employers seeking you out.

CHAPTER 4

Design a Workplace That Fits

In the next two sections of this book, we're going to look at a variety of settings you can end up in, whether that's an internship, a job, graduate school, or some other venture. But no matter where you land, you'll want to know that the setting you're in fits. And that's the purpose of this chapter. You've explored who you are and what you bring to the workplace (your interests, values, skills, and knowledge), so it's time to think about what you want from your workplace. What can the workplace offer you?

Designing My Ideal Work Situation

One thing we know about your skills and interests is that they are likely transferable. You can use them in a variety of settings. Have you ever had someone say, "You can do anything" with your major? It's meant to be a positive statement—the world is yours, so to speak. And to a certain extent it's true. You will be able to apply much of what you have learned in a variety of settings. That's the advantage of being a college student: you're just starting out and, while you know some things, you still have a lot to learn. You will learn a lot in your first job; in fact that's a goal for your first job—to learn. You can learn in a lot of different settings. So no matter what job you ultimately land in, mine it for everything. But back to that notion that you can do anything you want. First off, it's not completely true. I'm not sure your English degree teaches you how to design a structurally sound bridge. That's why this chapter and the next are so important. You need to define the parameters of the employment you're seeking.

It may seem odd that we're not jumping into lists of industries and job titles and all that, but you still have a little work to do. We'll look at industries and jobs in the next chapter. Before we look at specific industries that might influence your thinking, let's examine what you're seeking overall—the key elements of your ideal workplace or location. Even if you think you know the career you're seeking, chances are there are different environments where you can practice that career. This is your chance to think about all the factors that would make your future work as perfect as possible. Specifically we're going to examine four key elements that will help you clarify your ideal setting:

- The people you want to work with
- The type of setting you hope to work in
- The geographic location of your work
- The salary/benefits you hope to receive

My Preferred People: Identifying the People I Want to be With

No matter where you work (even if you work remotely), you likely will be communicating with someone. You will have colleagues with whom you interact daily, in person, online, or on the phone. You will attend meetings, work on teams, and be involved in projects. (By the way, this could lead you to a great interview question to ask a potential employer: "How much will I work independently and how much will I be part of a larger team?") Depending on the type of work you do, you will also likely have clients, customers, or even students.

Think about the various settings you've been in whether that's school, volunteering, interning, working, vacationing, or other.

When you think of your favorite types of people, what do you enjoy most?

What type of people appeal to you? Who are you naturally drawn to?

●●●

When Isabella answered these questions. she realized that it is most important for her to work around people who are creative and open-minded and interested in finding solutions to important issues. She believes she would be most comfortable with people who are focused on a cause or an issue that she cares about. She likes science and research and she thinks she would enjoy a medical-related setting. She wants to work around people who are more focused on doing the right thing, like finding a cure for a disease or developing a new medication, rather than making a lot of money.

Darius realized that he is most comfortable with people who set goals and are focused in their thinking. He wants to work with people who are committed to a cause, specifically racial justice. He wants an action-oriented environment where change can occur, not just conversations. He wants to know what kind of goals he would be expected to achieve in his work, and whether he would work with people who would have a can-do attitude and want to succeed with him. Competition doesn't bother him: he's played sports all his life. He understands the importance of both striving to do his personal best while at the same time making sure his teammates succeed, too. So he doesn't want a cut-throat, competitive environment, but at the same time he wants to be around other people who want to be successful, too.

Who Don't You Want to Be Around?

Another way Richard Bolles liked to think about the type of people you want to be around at work was to consider what you don't like about certain people. It may seem odd to focus on what we don't want, but sometimes focusing on the type of people we don't enjoy being around can help us identify what we do want.

To do this exercise, start by writing down various places where you've been around people. This could be in your school (high school or college), on summer jobs, at internships, in student organizations, or activities. Fill in Column 1 with those things. Then think about who you tended to avoid or who you found difficult to work with. (Sometimes you can even start with family members who are difficult.) Put the *characteristics* of those people (not their names!) in Column 2. Then in

Column 3, rank the characteristics you identified in Column 2, putting the worst traits at the top of your list. Now, in Column 4 consider what the opposite of that negative trait would be. For example, if you wrote that you disliked working with people who were gloomy, you might indicate in Column 4 you like people who are upbeat or optimistic. Give this exercise a try: you might be surprised at what you discover.

COLUMN 1	COLUMN 2	COLUMN 3	COLUMN 4
Settings where I've worked, volunteered, interned, or was part of an organization or group.	Kinds of people who annoyed me: describe their characteristics.	Rank the top five annoying characteristics of people I'd rather not work with.	Identify the opposite of the traits in column 3. What traits are you seeking in your colleagues, customers, or clients?

So here's the thing: you probably will find some of these less-than-desirable people no matter where you work. So one way to think about this section isn't so much about avoiding the random difficult person, but how you will overcome that situation.

- How will you work with them?
- How have you handled challenging people in the past?
- How were you able to get along well enough to accomplish the organization's goals?

Consider these questions carefully; they can be mined for great interview stories that demonstrate your ability to manage difficult conversations or situations.

Here's another way to think about the people you want to work with: their age. Use the following Thought Organizer to indicate what age ranges you would be most comfortable with. Check the box to the left of the age ranges you would enjoy working with in some capacity.

The Age-Range Thought Organizer

Gen Z: born 1996 to present. Includes a broad range of development, including preschool, elementary, and middle school children as well as high school and college students, and young adults.
Millennials or Gen Y: Born between 1977 and 1995
Generation X: Born between 1965 and 1976
Baby Boomers: Born between 1946 and 1964
Silent Generation: Born 1945 and earlier

As you consider these age groups, what are the services they will likely need? What are the typical problems or challenges associated with this age range? What products are they likely to buy? This may provide some ideas for possible careers that would let you work most often with the age range of interest. For instance, if you're interested in a career related to finance, you might consider the special financial needs of each age range and develop a specialty related to that.

An Exercise: Attending A Conference

You will likely have customers, colleagues, and clients no matter where you work or what you do. So let's start identifying the type of people you resonate with. Remember the Holland Code and the RIASEC exercise you did in chapter 1 when considering your major? Or in chapter 2 when focusing on your interests? Well, we're going to try that again. Now we're going to use Richard Bolles' "Party Exercise" to identify the type of people you would most enjoy working with.

The Party Exercise is based on Dr. John Holland's theories about the relationship between characteristics of workers and characteristics of the workplace. He believed that if you knew the type of work someone preferred, you would also know the type of people they would like to work with. And vice versa. He broke the workplace (and worker characteristics) into six people/environments categories, see page 78 for the breakdown. Most people aren't exclusively limited to one of these areas; in fact, it's common for people to have a combination of three types.

Richard Bolles invented a quick and easy way to discover which of the three types you are. Imagine you are at a professional gathering of successful people in their fields of work, and you get to choose which group of people you will approach. Which group would you approach first? Second? Third?

"Realistic"
People who have athletic or mechanical ability, prefer to work with objects, machines, tools, plants, or animals, or to be outdoors.

"Investigative"
People who like to observe, learn, investigate, analyze, evaluate, or solve problems.

"Conventional"
People who like to work with data, have clerical or numerical ability, carrying things out in detail, or following through on others' instructions.

"Artistic"
People who have artistic, innovative, or intuitional abilities, and like to work in unstructured situations, using their imagination or creativity.

"Enterprising"
People who like to work with people—influencing, persuading, performing, leading, or managing for organizational goals or for economic gain.

"Social"
People who like to work with people—to inform, enlighten, help, train, develop, or cure them, or are skilled with words.

R I C A E S

Write down your three top choices:

First choice: _____ **Second choice:** _____ **Third choice:** _____

What did you learn from this exercise? What type of people are you drawn to? How consistent are your choices when compared with your major and your interests noted earlier in this book? Are you starting to see a pattern, or are you finding that you are open to a lot of different types of people and experiences?

Now that you've had a chance to consider all sorts of people in the workplace, identify your top three to five preferences for the type of people you hope to work with, either as clients, customers, colleagues, or students:

1 _____

2 _____

3 _____

4 _____

5 _____

My Preferred Work Settings

Your physical setting can make a lot of difference in how you perform. Physical settings can cheer you up or drag you down. Under what conditions do you do your best work? Think back over your high school and college years. Do you need absolute quiet to focus? Or are you comfortable writing in a coffee shop with lots of ambient noise in the background? What setting do you need to be at your most effective?

As a college student, you may not have a lot of relevant work settings to draw on, but if you have had summer jobs or internships, volunteered, or otherwise had a chance to experience different work settings, take a moment to fill out this variation of a chart that Richard Bolles created. Think about the physical environment as well as the general setting (a bank, a store, an ice cream parlor, and so on). Don't focus on specific people you worked with, just the overall setting and style of the workplace. In column A indicate places where you have worked or volunteered. In column B jot down what you liked about the setting. This can be anything from "lots of windows and bright light" to "ergonomic work stations that were super-comfortable." (Remember this is about the setting, not the people.) Then in column C, write down anything you disliked about the setting ("cubicles instead of offices" or "no open spaces for conversations"). In column D, pull your thoughts together by listing your most important likes as well as what you disliked.

A PLACES I HAVE WORKED OR VOLUNTEERED:	B WHAT I LIKED ABOUT THE SETTING:	C WHAT I DISLIKED ABOUT THE SETTING:	D MOST IMPORTANT LIKES AND DISLIKES IN:

What did you learn about your preferences so far? How committed are you to them? For instance, if you discovered that you preferred a setting where you could work independently without a micromanaging boss, is that something you would like to keep seeking? Or if you preferred working closely with others, how important is that? Put a star next to what is most important to you. How important are the values of the organization you might work for? What values are most important to you and how might they be reflected by an organization?

Another way to think about this list, if you haven't had a chance to work in many settings, is to think about how you operate in school.

- Are you focused on organizations and other group activities, or do you tend to do things on your own or with just a few friends?
- Do you like high-action, lively activities and hobbies or are you more quiet?
- Are you enjoying your experience at a large school or would you prefer a smaller environment?
- Are you enjoying your experience at a small school or would you prefer a larger environment?

Here are some possible work settings. Try circling the ones that you would like to investigate further:

Airport	Bank	Casual office setting
College/university	Elementary school	Expensive/elegant office
Factory	Farm	Government agency
High school	Home-based/telecommute	Hospital/medical center
Industrial setting	Investment firm	Large corporation
Law firm	Middle school	Military
Nonprofit organization	Nursing home	New start-up
Outdoor setting	Police station	Public facility (tourism)
Rehabilitation center	Research (science) laboratory	Retail store
Small business	Social service agency	Technology-based company

Add additional settings you are interested in that aren't mentioned above:

If you circled any of the above, can you identify some sample organizations within that category that would interest you? For instance, if you selected "technology-based company," would that include places such as Google or Facebook? Or are you thinking about traditional companies, like Dell or IBM? Making a list of what interests you within that field or industry can be a great start to determining where you might want to work. If you're not sure, try searching the internet for a category, as in "Top Ten Retail Stores," and see what companies show up and why.

Keep in mind that most workplaces involve a trade-off. For instance, you might enjoy the thought of working for an interesting new start-up rather than a traditional company. The start-up likely offers creativity, flexible hours, a chance to build something from the ground up, promotion opportunities, and maybe even investment potential. The traditional company might not offer the same chance at creativity or flexibility due to more bureaucracy, but it might be more stable, provide more training, and offer a better retirement package. One isn't necessarily better than the other; they are just choices and you get to choose. You will want to consider what trade-offs you are willing to make. A company you like might be located in a city you don't like. How will you decide whether

Create a Vision Board of Your Ideal Workplace

A fun way to think about your workplace of the future is to create a vision board. Clip pictures from magazines or download them from the internet. Tack them onto a bulletin board or paste them onto a solid piece of cardboard. Include images of your location, work space, physical conditions, atmosphere, the geographic setting, even the clothes you'd like to wear. Use this activity as a way to think deeply about what is important to you and how you want to shape your life. What values are important to you in your workplace? How could you illustrate that through images? You can include images beyond the workplace: the place where you might live, images that suggest friends or family, hobbies, lifestyle choices, and so on. Adjust the board as you learn more about yourself and potential work settings.

to work there? Or a company might espouse a value or belief you don't endorse. You will want to decide what values or characteristics are most important to you and choose your future employer accordingly.

Basic Work Environments Thought Organizer

Here are some ways to think about your work environment. Based on your experiences so far and your general preference for a certain style of working, what are you looking for in a work setting? Look at these choices and consider what would be ideal for you. Circle the area that best fits your preferences and write a short explanation below each ranking.

1 Quiet & calm/ Casual-paced environment	2	3	4	5 Noisy & busy/ Fast-paced environment

My ideal: _____

1 Work alone on projects	2	3	4	5 Always in a team environment

My ideal: _____

1 Flexible hours/ schedule	2	3	4	5 Clear or fixed hours/schedule

My ideal: _____

1 Casual dress	2	3	4	5 Corporate/ Professional dress

My ideal: _____

_____

1 Creative/ Project-based	2	3	4	5 Controlled by corporate plans

My ideal: _____

_____

1 Organizational commitment to promote an anti-racist company culture	2	3	4	5 Organization with little commitment to diversity or inclusion

My ideal: _____

_____

Now that you have completed these exercises, summarize the type of work environment you prefer.

_____

_____

Describe the type of people you would like to work with.

_____

_____

Your Ideal Location: Geography and My Job Search

Another important consideration in your job search is your geographic location. Do you have a place in mind already? If so, write it down and you're done with this section! But if you are open to a lot of locations or haven't yet decided where you want to work, here are some exercises to help you make a decision.

- Where have you lived or visited? Make a list and rate them. Which ones would you return to?
- Are there places you already know you don't like?
- What is a dream location? How do you know about this? From a TV show? Can you find a way to visit there? How could you get a realistic picture of it?
- What are the industries in your area of interest?

If you haven't lived in or traveled to a variety of places, then this exercise may be more challenging to you. Work with what you know. What factors are important to you concerning where you live?

- Consider looking at medium-size cities. Many students head for the big cities such as New York and San Francisco, and they are terrific, but also very expensive. You might find that your paycheck will go further in a mid-size city. Try searching "most livable mid-size cities" online and see what locations are recommended.
- How do you hope to get to work: by car, bicycle, walking, or public transportation? You will want to investigate possible locations in terms of your ability to easily get around.
- Think about your hobbies. Are there locations where it would be easier to take part in your favorite activities?
- If you know the career field or industry you plan to work in, where are the best locations to start your career?
- Consider locations where you will find like-minded people and opportunities to interact with other people your age.
- What weather/climate are you hoping to experience?

How much access would you like to universities, cultural opportunities, and the like? If you're a huge Broadway fan, you might think about living in a city where you would have an opportunity to catch shows on tour (if you're not in New York City). Many medium-size cities sponsor the touring companies of shows. (And if you don't think you can afford the ticket prices, which is likely on a starting salary, you could volunteer as an usher or other assistant and catch the shows for free.) Remember, we're building a life here, not just finding a job.

Here's another thought: do you want to return home or not? Moving home has its benefits while you are getting your feet on the ground after college. If you know you want to (or need to) return home, you have a very specific geographic location to work with, one you already know. You're likely aware of the employment opportunities, major companies, or organizations located there. You already know some people in the community who may be able to help you. Former teachers, for example, may be thrilled to see that you are returning. You might even volunteer at your local high school to give a talk about the value of college to students who might need that motivational boost. Be sure to read pages 86 to 87 with information about moving home if that's an option for you.

My Ideal Island/ World Exercise

Want to create your own ideal geographic location? Here's a great exercise from Richard Bolles. He calls it "My Ideal Island/Ideal World." You can do this exercise by yourself or with friends if that would be more fun. Get a large piece of paper and draw an island. You decide how large or small your island is. Using words or simple drawings or symbols, start to include everything you'd like in this island. You can also make a list of what you don't want on your island (like pollution or lots of traffic). Consider these ideas about your island.

- **Weather:** What's the climate like? Tropical? Four seasons? Cold?
- **Nature:** Do you have mountains? Beaches? Volcanoes? Forests? Streams or rivers?
- **Human-made structures:** Buildings? Bridges? Roads? Rural? Towns? Cities?
- **Technology:** How advanced is the technology? State-of-the-art? Or none?
- **People:** Who lives on your island? What do they do? What are they like? What are their interests?
- **Family and friends:** Which family and friends are also on the island?
- **Activities:** What can you do on this island? Ski? Ride horses? Read books because you have the largest library in the world? Skateboard anywhere you want?
- **Stuff:** What's on the island? Restaurants? Shops? Types of businesses?
- **Values:** What's important to your island? Ecology/environment? Compassion for others? Religious focus?

Making the Most of Returning Home after Graduation

While planning your dream job on your ideal island, I'll bet your island wasn't located in your hometown. And yet, it is estimated that about 50 percent of college students return home after graduation.[6] You're not alone if you're returning home. Often a major motivator is money. It is expensive to move to a new city, pay rent, etc. In some cases, though, you might be expected to help out your family. This can be a challenge: you want to earn your money for yourself, but you just don't have that option. This is when it's time to develop a budget. Don't fall into the trap of "my parents pay for everything" so I don't need to save money. Quite the opposite. Unless living in your parent's home is your retirement plan, you will want to move out at some time. So start planning now. Even if you must share some of your paycheck with your family, always put away what you can for yourself. You must treat yourself fairly in this situation. Keep in mind that, yes, it's your home, but you are a guest or a tenant. You aren't a child anymore depending on your parents to do everything for you. Pitch in and help with whatever needs to be done at home. At home, you probably have a free or relatively cheap place to stay. Here are some tips for managing this:

- **Set goals for how long you plan to stay,** or what your game plan is for finding a job if you don't have one. Consider taking a temporary job simply to have your own income.

- **Open a bank account** if you don't already have one. Set up a savings plan from every paycheck. Even if you don't know the ultimate goal, having a pot of money is always helpful. It can help you afford a new car, graduate school or move to a new location.

- **Develop a budget and follow it.** Give yourself funds for a night or two out on the weekend, but keep it reasonable. The tendency is to splurge because you can—after all you're not paying rent, insurance, or other expenses.

- **Consider buying a car** if you're relying on your parents' car.

- **Consider working two jobs,** if necessary. You can use the money from one job to fill your bank account each week. Your goal is to create a fund that will allow you to eventually move out. For instance, maybe you work a standard nine-to-five job Monday through Friday, but then do something else (babysit, freelance work, teach an instrument, help people work their computers, and so on) to earn disposable income. That will allow you to save even more from your regular paycheck. You'll be amazed at how fast your account begins to build.

- **Pitch in and give back.** If your parents are letting you move home, that is a significant gift. Remember, they have probably been putting some of their lives on hold for years because of their children. Most parents are fine with this, but many do dream of the things they can do when their children are safely out of the house. They may have to put more things on hold (like vacations) when you return. So be grateful. Be appreciative. Offer to buy groceries or just fill up the fridge one day. Stop by a farmers' market and buy fresh vegetables for everyone to share. Stop at a bakery and bring home a cake just to celebrate. Without being asked, clean up. Not just your room but other rooms in the house.

- **Live by and with their rules,** and if you can't, move out.

Now that you have created your ideal world, start researching online to find out which real locations might actually come close to fitting what you need. You can Google phrases like "best places to live for college graduates," or "best places to live in the South," or "best climates to live in" based on whatever your criteria might be.

My Ideal Salary and Benefits

In general, salaries are based on several factors: the title of the position, the responsibilities of the position, the employment sector and field, and the geographic location. As someone new in your profession, you have less ability to negotiate. Certainly, you can try (see tips in chapter 9) but many organizations have a fixed salary or wage for entry-level positions.

You may or may not have kept a budget so far in your life. But figuring out a budget for your future spending is a great way to get a handle on the funds you will need to support yourself once you're out of college. We all think we know how much money we need to earn. But one of the best ways to really know is by making a budget. On page 90 you will find a simple guide to the categories you need to think about. Figure out what you think you will need on a monthly basis in each category. If you see any categories missing, do not hesitate to add them.

One way to start looking at how you spend money is to keep a simple list of your daily expenses.

For one month, write down every penny you spend—whether that's in cash or on a credit card. Note everything from food to clothes to books. Yes, that cup of coffee in the morning counts. Everything. You can just jot down notes at the end of each day, but lots of apps make this task much easier. For example, there is Spending Tracker, Pocket Expense, Goodbudget, and, for all those who want to sync with their bank accounts, Mint.com. The good news: All are simple, and all are free.

At the end of the month, look over your spending.

- How much was imperative? What did you have to spend to live? That might include rent or housing, food, and books for school. If you have a car, include any gas or insurance costs.

- How much was discretionary? What did you spend on that extra pizza or the cup of coffee?

- Total up the imperative spending and see how much money you need each month just for basic survival.

- Then total up the discretionary funds to get an idea of how you would like to live. Once you have a monthly total, you will have a general idea of how much you will need in monthly income. Note: if you anticipate you'll be paying student loans after your graduate, check with your financial aid office to see how much your monthly bill will be. You must add that into your monthly expenses.

- Finally, assume that about 25 percent of your paycheck will be removed for items such as taxes, FICA, and health care. So if you discovered you need $3,000 each month for necessities, you will actually need at least $3,750 per month or $45,000 per year to cover your expenses. If you're looking at hourly wages, you will need about $23.45/hour.

- Try calculating both your survival (necessity) budget for the year and your ideal budget (to allow for a vacation and perhaps all the pizza and coffee you want!) and see what the difference is. That will give you the range of salary you need.

On the following pages is a chart to help you get started on the expenses you can expect after graduation. If you're not sure how much something will cost, research the information online. Just draw a line through any expenses that don't apply to you. Where you have a range of options, put the survival amount in that column and the ideal amount in the other.

MONTHLY EXPENSES	MINIMUM (SURVIVAL)	MAXIMUM (IDEAL)
Housing		
Rent or mortgage payments		
Electricity/Gas		
Water		
Phone/Internet		
Garbage removal		
Cleaning, maintenance, repairs		
Food		
What you spend at the grocery store		
Eating out (include coffee)		
Clothing		
Purchase new or used clothing		
Cleaning, dry cleaning, laundry		
Automobile/transportation		
Car payments		
Gas		
Repairs		
Public transportation (bus, train)		
Uber/Lyft		
Insurance		
Car		
Medical or health care		
House and personal possessions		
Life		
Taxes		
Federal (divide total by 12)		
State (divide total by 12)		
Local (divide total by 12)		
Property (divide total by 12)		

MONTHLY EXPENSES	MINIMUM (SURVIVAL)	MAXIMUM (IDEAL)
Medical expenses		
Doctors' visits		
Prescriptions		
Fitness costs (gym, yoga, etc.)		
Supporting others		
Child care		
Child support		
Support for your parents (if you're helping out)		
Charity giving or church tithe		
Other Expenses to Consider		
Continuing education (grad school, etc.)		
Student loans		
Pet care		
Credit cards		
Other obligations paid monthly		
Savings		
Monthly savings contribution		
Retirement contribution		
Amusement/discretionary spending		
Movies, Netflix, etc.		
Other kinds of entertainment		
Subscriptions		
Gifts (birthdays, holidays, etc.)		
Vacations		
Other Expenses		
Total Amount You Need Each Month		

Now that you have a general idea of the salary range you will need after you graduate, you should also look into the benefits an employer can offer you. Sometimes the benefit package can be almost as important as the salary itself, because good benefits can reduce the amount of money you have to spend on things such as insurance or health care. Here are some sample benefits you might be offered. Which ones would you likely use or appreciate? Which ones are imperative to you?

You may wish to list other rewards, besides money, that you would hope for from your next job or career. Check the benefits you will want to research. Keep in mind that few companies will offer all of these, so decide what your minimum benefits package will need to be.

RESEARCH	POSSIBLE BENEFITS
	Ability to telecommute
	Child care benefits
	Commuting assistance
	Company car
	Dental insurance
	Gym memberships or discounts
	Health insurance
	Life insurance
	Low-cost or free meals
	Paid time off (PTO) for illness and vacations
	Relocation assistance
	Retirement benefits
	Short-term and long-term disability insurance
	Student loan repayment
	Tuition reimbursement
	Vision insurance
	Wellness programs

Revisit Your Values

Before we leave this chapter, let's revisit the values you listed at the end of chapter 2. See if you want to add anything now that you've examined possible work characteristics. You've analyzed the people you want to be around, the physical conditions you might work in, and the salary you might earn. Are there other factors that would be important to you in the workplace? Here's a list to consider. Mark the ones that appeal to you and add more as needed.

Would you like a chance to:

- Be a leader
- Be challenged
- Be creative
- Be part of an inclusive and diverse environment
- Be intellectually stimulated
- Be physically active
- Be popular
- Be respected
- Find adventure
- Find fame
- Have power
- Help others
- Influence others
- Make decisions
- Use your expertise

Finding Your Fit When You Have a Disability

Finding your fit requires that you know who you are (your strengths, your challenges, your potential) and then finding the work setting where you will thrive. As a bright college student, you might also have some medical conditions such as visual or hearing impairments, mobility challenges, ADHD, learning disabilities, autism, Tourette's syndrome, or mood disorders. Each of these conditions presents challenges to everyday life as well as the job search and the workplace. But there is no one "typical" person with these issues. Just because you have autism, for example, does not necessarily mean that a career in computers is for you. It's a possibility, of course, but you will need to do the exercises in the first two chapters of this book to get a full picture of your strengths before you pigeonhole yourself into a career field. You will need to know your own personal pattern of strengths and interests in order to find the best work environment. Completing the exercises in chapters 2 and 3 will help immensely with this process.

Whatever your situation is, it's important to find allies: people who can help and support you. Throughout your time in college, be on the lookout for people who get you—people who understand your needs and your gifts. These individuals could include your professors, residence hall advisors, career center staff, counseling center staff, and, of course, the disabilities services office.

Consider speaking with a career coach at your career center about your situation. If you will need accommodations in the interview process, your coach can assist you. You are probably an expert already in how to accommodate your situation in school. You (hopefully) have worked with your disability services office and received any necessary classroom accommodations. Perhaps you even selected your major based on your strengths or skills, while avoiding majors that wouldn't bring out your best performance. This self-knowledge will help you with planning your potential career.

Your coach can also help you identify careers and workplace settings that would take advantage of your gifts. For instance, it's not unusual for individuals who have had to interact with the health care system their whole lives to choose a medical-related career. And if that's what you're thinking, a career coach can help guide you to the best specialty that fulfills your interests and values.

As you think about a workplace, where would you most likely thrive? Do you relish a fast-paced environment, or do you have sensory overload issues and need a calm, quiet setting? Do you want to be surrounded by people, or would you prefer to work alone? Should the environment be constantly changing or stable? Pay special attention to the Basic Work Environments Thought Organizer on page 82 to get a clear picture of the best environment for your success.

Also, what modifications or technology would help you succeed in the workplace? Do you need wheelchair access? Will you need special computer adaptations for visual or auditory issues? If you have difficulty with organization, what currently keeps you organized? Do you use an online calendar or your cell phone to keep track of your schedule? You can continue to do this at work—in fact, you can use this as an example in your interview. If you're asked about a "greatest weakness" (a common interview question), you could bring up the challenge of keeping yourself organized. And then you can explain how you have overcome this by using whatever technique you use.

If you are neurodiverse, a proper work setting can make all the difference in your career success. It's not unusual for individuals diagnosed with ADHD to like a stimulating environment with lots of activity where they don't have to sit for hours at a time. Individuals with ADHD often do well in action-oriented careers, like sports, entertainment, emergency room doctor or nurse, international journalist, and so on. Creative settings can work well, too. Opportunities to travel and experience new environments such as one might find in consulting might be a good fit for you. Working outdoors is another option; many individuals with ADHD function better in an outdoor environment.

If you have a diagnosis of autism, again, consider what environments allow you to succeed. Are you strong at focusing on one task for hours at a time? Are you good at logical puzzles or computer programming? Do you enjoy repetitive tasks, like cataloging or data entry? All those areas offer potential employment opportunities. You might also want to investigate freelance work or remote work settings where you won't have to interact with lots of people. Individuals with autism often find successful careers in areas such as accounting, computers, technology, engineering, or mechanical fields. But this is just a general guide; the better you know yourself, the better fit you will find.

continued →

These are topics you will need to discuss with your employer either during the interview process or after the offer is made. Legally, you are not required to disclose a disability. But, practically, it can make sense to bring up any disabilities that are visible so that you can have an honest conversation with the potential employer. Let the employer know what your strengths and talents are so that they see beyond any physical limitation. If you focus on your strengths and how well you have adapted so far, so will they. In fact, many large corporations already have strong support programs for people with disabilities. Lately, companies have been developing specific career programs for neurodiverse individuals. You can usually find information about an organization's programs for people with disabilities on their website. Take note of whether they just have the official non-discrimination language or whether they appear to have support programs and other services. Thoroughly review the human resources section of their website to uncover these opportunities. You can also find listings of the top employers for people with disabilities by going online and searching "Careers and the Disabled Top 50."

Whatever your personal situation is, know that the Parachute System will work for you—you may just need to modify certain activities. For instance, if you are more comfortable talking on the phone, you might want to conduct your information interviews that way. Or you might be more comfortable with an email exchange. Again, what you need to do is focus on what works best for you and what accommodations you need to create to succeed. Plan to work closely with your career center and the disability services office at your college for guidance.

And Now . . . You're Ready to Pack Your Backpack

Let's create the final picture of you and the type of work environment you're seeking. Have you done everything to pack your Backpack for this trip? If not, consider going back. Think of it this way, if anything is missing from your Backpack, it's going to be harder to make the trip. If there's a hole in your parachute, it will be a little harder to land. If you're coming in for a landing, the stronger your parachute is and the fuller your Backpack, the more likely you'll be successful in landing where you want to.

My Backpack Profile

My key interests I'd like to apply to a future career are:	The value and purpose this would support is:
The top skills I can offer an employer are:	The knowledge I have that will be valued is:
I would like to work with these types of people:	I would like to work in this part of the country/world:
I would like this type of work setting:	I'd prefer a salary in the range of:
I am most interested in this type of work:	Other items I need to include in my Backpack:

Part 2

Take Off

Parachute into Your Future

This section will help you develop your plans and design the communications to connect you to your future.

Survey the Landscape and Decide Where to Land

On a recent flight from Tennessee to Arizona, my plane was flying at a low enough altitude to see the ground below. I noticed these perfectly shaped bright green circles on the ground. Some were quite large, others smaller, and their shades of green varied. They were clearly marked and—if I'd had a parachute—they would have made great targets for landing. (I looked them up: they are pivot irrigation circles.) And as I surveyed the immense landscape with its many landing circles, I realized this was a perfect metaphor for what you are doing in college. You are up there in the plane deciding where you want to parachute to. Into which of these attractive circles would you like to land?

That's what this book is ultimately about: the many choices you have for creating a future that fits.

So how do you start thinking about where you want to land? Here are some ideas:

- Keep in mind that you are still growing and learning. No landing has to be permanent. You are trying things out. The more you try out, the more you will learn.

- By completing the exercises in the previous chapters, you already have a head start on the decision-making process. You have a lot of self-knowledge that will help you navigate your trip.
- Your choices often represent your best guess.
- Where you land can be as much a result of chance as it is choice. You can design a plan that looks great on paper, but life has a way of intervening.
- This is actually good news, because it means if you have a plan, you can start following it today. But if you don't have a plan, you can just experiment and try stuff until something clicks.

So let's look at how you can start making preliminary decisions about where you want to land—what you want to do next based on what you currently know. Once you have some possible landing ideas, you can then use the information in the next few chapters to connect with others who can help you learn more. And as you learn more, you'll adjust your plans accordingly. This process can be seen as an ongoing interaction between making a choice (a decision) and then learning.

The Choice/Learning Process

Let's make something clear about the career decision-making and the job-search process: predictions are unreliable. Whether you are relying on the RIASEC/Holland Code, or the cool career you saw on a TV show, or the career your parents think you should do, or even all the work you did in the first few chapters, it's all a guess. Some guesses are better informed than others, which is why they make better predictors. That's why knowing yourself, getting direct experience, and building your knowledge and network is so important. The more you know, the better you will be at guessing.

We can't predict with 100 percent accuracy what career you'll be in, or what careers will be hot (or cold) in five years. So take that pressure off. Instead, focus on what works for now, what your best guess is at this moment, how sure you are about that guess, and move forward. Keep an open mind and keep learning. In fact, let's look more closely at the concept of learning.

As you look at your options and continue to meet people and try new experiences, focus on what you are learning, what you have learned, and what you can learn. Here's an extremely simple way to think about your future planning process:

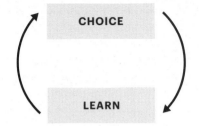

As the diagram illustrates, you start with a choice. Maybe your choice is to take on a particular internship or a job. And you do that. Once you've made that choice, you move toward it.

Whether through actually doing that choice, or simply learning more about it, you discover it was a great choice. And so you keep going and you stay in the job, or you use the internship to find a job. Or you pursue the necessary education. Regardless, you stay in that career field. Eventually you have an opportunity to move up in the field, and you choose to do that, too.

OR

Maybe you make a choice and you learn that it wasn't the right one for you. You thought you would enjoy a career field, and now you don't. Through your research you learned a lot that has now turned you off. Or you did an internship in what you thought was your dream job, and you didn't like it at all. So you analyze: what's wrong?

One thing you might discover is that the better-paying jobs are often less desirable. Sometimes the higher salary reflects the knowledge or education needed. But sometimes the high pay represents long hours or difficult work conditions. And sometimes the most popular jobs don't pay as well because everyone wants them. So if you're being influenced by an unusually high salary, you might want to look into that.

You might also learn that job titles aren't always accurate. A term like "consultant" can be vague; you can be a "beauty consultant" and end up behind the makeup counter at a pharmacy. That's probably not what you had in mind. Same thing with marketing. You're thinking about developing a marketing campaign or finding a unique brand for a product, but it turns out the marketing job is really a sales position for a product that's hard to sell. Or marketing can sometimes mean you're in a grocery store arranging your product on their shelves. Now those positions are perfectly fine for the right person. But they might not be the marketing position you had in mind. That's why investigating beyond the job title is so important.

When you're analyzing career fit and making your choices, try considering what the government focuses on in the Occupational Outlook Handbook (https://www.bls.gov/ooh). For every career, they look at what the specific duties are, what the typical work environments are, the steps involved in entering and moving upward in the career, the typical salaries and job titles for the positions, the job outlook for the future, and what alternative similar careers might exist. By applying these guidelines to the career field you are considering, you are well on the way to making a good choice.

Consider making a list to clarify your thoughts about the choices you have made so far. Even if you abandoned a previous career choice, chances are your initial choice or plan wasn't completely wrong—there were probably parts of your experience you liked. And parts of that experience fit something you were seeking. List those in the first column.

You are probably aware of aspects you didn't like, so list them in the second column. Finally, use the third column to list what you think you would prefer in your next job, internship, or experience.

WHAT WAS RIGHT ABOUT MY CHOICE?	WHAT DIDN'T I LIKE ABOUT MY CHOICE?	WHAT WOULD I PREFER NOW?

Where does your new knowledge lead? What have you now learned from this list? It's really that simple. You make a choice, you try it out, you learn, and then react accordingly.

Just be aware that the first step is to make a choice. You must decide on something and try it out. If you spend all your time pondering and not really trying anything out, you won't have the opportunity to learn. Always opt for learning.

As you now go further into the Parachute approach, keep these important concepts in mind:

- **You are in charge.** Not the employer. Not the job market. You are always making choices. Yes, they can be influenced by what's happening in the world, but you are still making the choice based on your knowledge, your research, and your own determination of the right fit.

- **You determine your "dream job"** as Richard Bolles calls it. What factors would constitute your dream job?

- **You maintain self-awareness.** You decide what fits you and what doesn't. For instance, job market predictions might be telling you that health care and technology are two great fields for future employment. And they are. So you might want to see how your talents and interests could fit into those fields. Or you might decide that those areas simply don't interest you and seek a better fit elsewhere.

- **You use the talents and knowledge of other people** to keep expanding your own knowledge to make better choices in the future.

- **You keep your focus on your strengths** and find ways to work around your weaknesses.

Use Your Backpack to Start Generating Ideas

Let's start your career decision-making by reviewing the last page of the chapter you just completed—your Backpack Profile of skills, interests, and knowledge. As you review what you learned about yourself, what careers do you think seem to fit your pattern?

CAREER IDEAS
1
2
3
4
5

Share your profile with others and ask them what careers come to mind when they see your pattern of interests, skills, and knowledge. Who could help you with this activity?

- Friends
- Relatives

- Career coach
- Counselor
- Professor
- Minister
- People you admire and whose opinion you respect
- Alumni from your high school and college
- Someone in your field of interest

Did your conversations yield anything valuable? Do you have some career fields or job titles to consider? Take the time to research them online and then in person. If you have some ideas already, you might want to jump to the next chapter and start working on your resume and developing a network related to your career interests. If this exercise didn't yield good results, keep reading.

Generating Ideas: Expanding and Narrowing Your Career Options

Richard Bolles created a great diagram that illustrates how the career decision-making process works. It provides a perfect way to start thinking about where you want to land. It is two triangles, with one expanding and the other contracting.

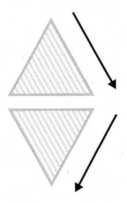

The process of career decision-making is about starting out with your ideas (which might be limited by what you currently know) and expanding them as you learn more about yourself and more about the employment world. Then gradually honing your ideas until you reach the list of opportunities that best fit you.

Here's a way to use this diagram. Start by selecting a skill you're good at and you enjoy using. Then think about all the ways you could apply that skill to specific tasks or job duties.

• • •

Anthony loves to write. He's been writing for fun ever since he wrote his first science-fiction short story in middle school. He enjoys writing papers for his college classes and even became known in his residence hall as the go-to guy for help with papers. It's a skill he is confident about, and he'd like to continue developing it. So as he thinks about how he might apply his writing skills at work, he brainstorms a list of ideas.

1 *A professional blogger?*
2 *Investigative reporter for an online, on air, or print news outlet?*
3 *Research writer for a foundation or think tank?*
4 *Research/analysis expert for a government agency?*
5 *Grant writer for a nonprofit organization?*
6 *Policy researcher/writer for a political cause or campaign?*
7 *Researcher, writing articles for professional journals?*
8 *Editor for a book publisher, magazine, or online publication?*
9 *Freelance writer or editor?*
10 *Novelist?*
11 *Librarian or archives researcher?*
12 *Writing professor or teacher?*

Each of these ideas leads him in a different direction. Some might require further education; all will likely require experience through a job or internship. He has a dream of someday being a novelist, but he also knows he needs to pay off some student loans. He likes the security of a paycheck, and he decides freelancing is too risky. So, like his favorite author, John Grisham, he will get a job and write his first novel in his spare time. He found an excellent book on careers in publishing (The Insider's Guide to a Career in Book Publishing by Carin Siegfried), and he started researching his other career ideas on the internet, looking up job descriptions on sites such as Indeed.com. From his research and self-analysis, he realizes he doesn't want just a generic writing or editing job. In addition to writing, his next favorite interest is politics. He's decided to look for opportunities where he can research and write about policy issues. He now knows he's going to pursue career ideas 2, 3, 4, and 6. By focusing on his interests in addition to his strength as a writer, he will be able to better clarify how he might use his writing skills in a way that will add value to his life.

•••

If you haven't done so already, try this exercise. Start with what interests you most. Take the core of what you enjoy and expand the fields into possible jobs. And then start to narrow it back down as you determine what interests you and what doesn't.

What if you have two or three interests or several skills you want to use? Remember Ashley from the Introduction (page 1)? If you recall, she's the student who plays the banjo and is also studying neuropsychology. Just like Anthony, she made a list of possible career options based on her two key interests. She decided to look at each area separately and then brainstorm creative ways to combine her interests. Here's what she came up with:

MUSIC CAREER IDEAS	NEUROPSYCHOLOGY CAREER IDEAS	COMBINATION CAREERS
Professional musician in a band or as a solo act	PhD in cognitive science or related fields	PhD focusing on cognition and music
Manage arts program in museum or gallery	Medical degree	Neuropsychologist specializing in music-related learning
Certified music teacher	College professor	Music therapist
Manager/agent for musicians	Research scientist at a university or private laboratory	Using music as wellness/mindfulness/stress reduction coach or counselor
Booking manager for a performance venue	Licensed psychologist in private practice	App developer related to music as a cognitive enhancement for children
Start nonprofit music festival or programs	Specialize in sports injuries or related head injuries	Rehabilitation therapist or counselor using arts
Administer music programs in higher-ed setting	Specialize in autism or other neurodevelopment issues	Design education programs teaching music (songwriting) for veterans with PTSD
Create short lessons on YouTube that people can subscribe to	Work at a medical rehabilitation center	Design online intro to music training for parents of neurodiverse children
Teach professional online music classes through Skype	Therapist in a hospital or private setting	Play/arts therapist in hospital or clinical setting

continued →

MUSIC CAREER IDEAS	NEUROPSYCHOLOGY CAREER IDEAS	COMBINATION CAREERS
Music merchandising	Addictions specialist	Music cognition laboratory researcher
Public relations for music venue	Cognitive, clinical, forensic, or pediatric neuropsychologist	Data analyst for music marketing and advertising firm

Do you see how her world of career possibilities has opened up just by examining two key interests? Just like Anthony, she can focus on her specific skills, the knowledge she currently has and wants to acquire, and her values to determine what the best setting might be for her career.

Now you try this. Write down three key skills you hope to use in your future career:

1 _____

2 _____

3 _____

Now write down three key interests you would also like to have in your future work:

1 _____

2 _____

3 _____

Now try combining them in as many creative ways you can. If you're stuck, ask your friends and family. Read books and websites specifically devoted to your career field. Learn as much as you can about the industry and the job titles. Doing your research now will make you stand out to interviewers when you tackle the next chapters on starting conversations and writing your resume. Take a basic vision for your future and expand it.

Do you have a plan now? Are you ready to move on to making connections and gaining experience? Then head on to the next chapters.

Still not sure? There are more ways to think about what to do next. Here's a creative way to think about your career.

Thinking About Jobs? Look Behind The Scenes

Anything that interests you contains hidden job opportunities. Take anything you like and ask yourself, "What jobs are behind this product or service? Who is responsible for its creation?" You might be surprised to learn the many jobs connected to whatever interests you.

For instance, have you ever sat through the credits at the end of a movie or TV show and realized just how many people were employed in the process? We tend to think about key roles, like the actors or the director, but there are many other jobs related to a television or film production.

That Netflix series you just finished required a whole chain of individuals to bring it to the screen. It likely started with an idea from a writer who had to develop the characters, plot, story, and script. The writer probably had an agent to promote the concept and script. Someone had to read the script and greenlight the project. A producer had to be involved to bring the project together. Lawyers were needed to represent everyone throughout the production, write contracts, secure trademarks and copyrights, license merchandise, and so on. The production company probably put the whole project together from the producers to directors, set designers, continuity specialists, makeup artists, editors, prop managers, and all the other crew members. If the project involved animation (think titles and closing credits), CGI specialists and animators were hired. And then there was music somewhere along the way, so that's more people who either compose the music, perform it, edit it, and so on. If animals were involved, there were animal wranglers and a representative from American Humane. Depending on the location of the production, many of these jobs were union jobs, so the pay was usually good. Someone had to publicize the show or no one would have known about it. Posters and promotional materials had to be created, advertisements developed, and all sent out. The list of jobs related to a production like this is almost endless. And keep in mind, many of these positions have assistants or interns, so there could be some excellent early career/learning opportunities related to a production.

Another quick way to discover jobs related to your interests is to select a magazine related to a topic you enjoy and start reading articles about what takes place behind the scenes. In addition to the obvious need for writers and photographers, you can uncover other hidden careers. Start by looking at the editorial listing. You'll find everything from acquisition editor to art director to circulation manager. But beyond that, look at the advertisements in the magazine. The products are likely items you might consider purchasing or have an interest in. For example, a sports magazine will advertise everything from athletic equipment to clothing to medical-related products for treating injuries. There might be an ad for a travel company that offers special sports-related tours, or a facility that provides sports training or therapy. Starting with your simple interest in sports, you can uncover a wealth of careers that might fit you.

Even your favorite hair product can be a potential resource. Look at the label to see who manufactures it. Check out that company's website. Look them up on Indeed.com to see if they have any jobs posted. Check to see if an alumnus works for the company. You might find that your interest in the product makes you the perfect brand manager, marketer, or salesperson for it. You might be interested in supply chain or manufacturing or product development. Or if you lean toward the sciences, you might be able to work in quality control, the laboratory that develops the formulas, or elsewhere.

So use your Backpack items to determine which roles in these industries interest you and fit you best. Here's a cheat sheet for finding some of these hidden opportunities.

- Make a list of your favorite products, particularly those related to favorite hobbies or interests.

- Look behind the scenes. Read the background information: the credit reel, the editing masthead, the "about us" section of a company website.

- Check out the company online—beyond their website. Read reviews of the company from other sites, like Glassdoor (https://www.glassdoor.com/index.htm). Find their LinkedIn page. See who works there and what their titles are. Jot down the job titles that sound interesting to you.

- Look for alumni who work in the industry or company you're seeking.

- Find jobs on Indeed, LinkedIn, at the company site. Look specifically for internships, summer jobs, or entry-level positions where you could learn.

Meta-Careers: Career Industries

So you've tried brainstorming (with yourself and others), considered a dream job, and looked for a hidden career, but you're still stuck? Let's try another approach.

When most people think about the job sector, they divide it into broad categories, like for-profit (business), nonprofit, or government. It's important to remember that all these sectors have similar job titles and descriptions. You can be an educator and work for the government (teacher in a public school system, trainer in the military) or the for-profit sector (training in any industry) or for a nonprofit (a college or private school, for example). So as you can see, it's more helpful to focus first on the actual work you want to do and then decide which sector offers the best opportunities and fit for you.

Remember in the first chapter when we discussed meta-majors: those groupings of various majors into overall families or clusters? You can do the same thing with careers. We call them *industries*. There are hundreds of industries (just like there are hundreds of majors) but we can sort industries into meta-industries. Here are fifteen meta-industries that most careers and jobs can be sorted into:

Business administration/management/sales/consulting
Communications/advertising/marketing/public relations/journalism
Computing/information technology
Education/social services/psychological services
Engineering/manufacturing/construction/transportation
Environment/energy/animals/farming
Finance/banking
Fine arts/crafts/design/architecture
Government/politics/military
Health care/medical/pharmaceutical
Law/security/emergency services
Nonprofit/NGO
Performing arts/entertainment
Science/research/technology
Sports/leisure/tourism

As you read through this list, does one meta-industry sector appeal to you? Place a check next to it. Are you interested in several? Check them as well. Consider ordering them by preference to determine which field you'd like to investigate first.

Keep in mind that these are broad breakdowns, and many specific careers and job titles could overlap into different industry classifications. For instance, a career in "design" could be in technology, fine arts, or interior design.

On the next few pages you will see lists of sample job titles under each of the meta-industry categories.

Read through the titles and circle the ones that interest you.

- Don't think about salary or whether you're qualified; just circle the ones that sound like you might enjoy them as a career.

- Understand that many of the job titles have lower-level, yet related positions. For instance, many scientist positions have "technician" roles that don't require the same level of training that the named role requires. A chemistry technician role will not require the same education as the chemist role. You can often get a foot in the door of a desired organization or field by taking a more entry-level position.

- Many general job titles have lots of variations and specialties. Attorneys can be broken down by specialties such as intellectual property, real estate, litigator, environmental, patent, and so on. Psychologists can specialize in children, adults, substance abuse, research, industrial/organizational, and more. And with "teacher" the list is practically endless. You can teach any age from preschool to adult. You can teach in virtually every subject area from business to zoology. You can teach special education or vocational education. So if you selected one of these broad career titles, look them up to learn about the various specialties that might interest you.

Here are sample job titles broken down by meta-industry:

Business (including business administration, management, sales, and consulting)

Accountant	Account Manager	Actuary
Auditor	Business analyst	Business development director
Business owner	Business strategy consultant	Buyer

Business (including business administration, management, sales, and consulting—continued)

Career coach and consultant	Chief executive officer	Data analyst
Demonstrator and product promoter	Entrepreneur	Event planner
Human resources director	Human resources specialist	Inside sales representative
Insurance sales agent	Management consultant	Manager
Medical biller or coder	Operations manager	Outside sales representative
Project manager	Real estate broker	Real estate developer
Real estate sales agent	Restaurant manager	Retail salesperson
Risk manager	Sales manager	Sales representative
Sales supervisor	Social media manager	Software consultant
Store manager	Strategy consultant	Supply chain manager

Communications (including advertising, journalism, marketing, media, and PR)

Account executive	Advertising sales agent	Art director
Assistant editor	Author	Brand manager
Broadcaster	College alumni and development officer	Communications manager
Communications specialist	Copywriter	Editor
Editorial assistant	Electronic marketing manager	Graphic artist/ web designer
Investigative reporter	Journalist	Marketing consultant
Marketing manager	Marketing research analyst	Marketing specialist
Media buyer	Media director	Media planner
Meeting/event planner	Merchandising manager	News analyst
Product manager	Proofreader	Public relations specialist
Publicist	Reporter	Social media assistant
Social media manager	Telecommunications specialist	Television announcer

Computing/Information Technology

Computer hardware engineer	Computer network architect	Computer programmer
Computer scientist	Computer software designer	Computer support specialist
Computer systems analyst	Computer user support specialist	Database administrator
Database architect	Data scientist	High-tech sales
Information security analyst	IT consultant	Java developer
Malware analyst	Mathematician	Network architect
Operations research analyst	Software and web developer	Software and web programmer
Software and web tester	Software quality assurance analyst	Statistician
Technical writer	Web and digital interface designer	Webmaster

Education/Social Services/Psychological Services

Academic advisor	Addiction counselor	Adult education specialist
Anthropologist	Archaeologist	Archivist
Behavior analyst	Career counselor	Case worker
Clergy	Clinical psychologist	College admissions counselor
College professor	Community health worker	Conservator
Correctional treatment specialist	Counselor	Curator
Economist	Education administrator	Employment interviewer
Employment recruiter	English as a second language instructor	Exercise trainer
Exhibit designer	Family/marriage therapist	Geographer
Health education specialist	Historian	Instructional coordinator
Librarian	Market and survey researcher	Marriage and family therapist

Education/Social Services/Psychological Services (continued)

Mediator	Medical case manager	Medical/public health social worker
Museum conservator	Museum technician	Music therapist
Nanny	Occupational therapist	Palliative and hospice care social worker
Political scientist	Probation officer	Psychologist
Psychotherapist	Recreation and fitness worker	Religious activities and education director
Religious leader	Social worker	Sociologist
Substance abuse specialist	Survey researcher	Teacher
Teacher assistant	Technical writer	Trainer
Tutor	Urban and regional planner	Youth counselor

Engineering/Manufacturing/Construction/Transportation

Aerospace engineer	Agricultural engineer	Agricultural inspector
Arborist	Architect	Architectural and civil drafter
Automotive engineer	Bioengineer	Biomedical engineer
Calibration technologist and technician	Cartographer	Chemical engineer
Civil engineer	Computer engineer	Computer hardware engineer
Drafter	Electrical and electronics drafter	Electrical engineer
Electro-mechanical technologist	Energy auditor	Engineer
Engineering technician	Engineering technologist	Environmental engineer
Environmental engineering technologist	Health and safety engineer	Industrial engineer
Landscape architect	Mapping technician	Marine engineer
Materials engineer	Materials science engineer	Mechanical drafter
Mechanical engineer	Mechanical engineering technologist	Mining and geological engineer

continued →

Engineering/Manufacturing/Construction/Transportation (continued)

Mining safety engineer	Mining safety inspector	Naval architect
Nuclear engineer	Petroleum engineer	Photogrammetrist
Software engineer	Surveying and mapping technician	Surveyor

Environment/Energy/Animals/Farming

Agricultural scientist	Agricultural technician	Animal behaviorist
Animal scientist	Aquatic ecologist	Biological monitor assistant
Chief sustainability officer	Climatologist	Conservation scientist
Conservation technician	Environmental analyst	Environmental attorney
Environmental field consultant	Environmental investigator	Environmental planner
Environmental scientist	Environmental specialist	Environmental technician
Field service technician	Food scientist	Geoscientist
Gis analyst	Humane educator	Humane law enforcement
Hydrologist	Industrial hygienist	Landscape architect
Leed-accredited design professional	Meteorologist	Solar technician
Sustainability advocate	Urban planner	Veterinarian
Veterinary assistant	Veterinary technologist	Wetland scientist
Wildlife biologist	Wind turbine technician	Zoologist

Finance/Banking

Accountant	Actuary	Banking regulator
Bank manager/ vice-president	Bankruptcy coordinator	Bank teller
Branch manager	Budget analyst	Commercial real estate agent
Credit analyst	Customer service representative	Financial advisor
Financial analyst	Financial consultant	Financial planner

Finance/Banking (continued)

Financial services sales agent	Investment banker	Investor relations specialist
Loan officer	Loan underwriter	Manager of a stock/bond/mutual fund
Securities and commodities sales agent	Stockbroker	Treasurer

Fine Arts (including crafts, design, and architecture)

Agent	Animator	Architect
Art and design worker	Art director	Artist
Augmented reality design	Author	Choreographer
Commercial and industrial designer	Commercial art gallery manager	Community arts worker
Copywriter	Cosmetologist	Craftsperson
Curator	Dancer	Design architect
Designer	Digital artist	Fashion designer
Film and video editor	Film director	Film editor
Fine artist	Floral designer	Game designer
Graphic designer	Hairstylist	Illustrator
Interior designer	Medical illustrator	Merchandise displayer/window trimmer
Mobile designer (apps)	Multimedia artist	Painter
Photographer	Printmaker	Sculptor
Set and exhibit designer	Simultaneous captioner	UX Designer
Videographer	Visual designer	Writer

Government/Politics/Military

Accountant	Air traffic controller	Arbitrator
Attorney	Border patrol agent	Community organizer and activist
Consultant	Correctional officer	Court reporter
Criminal investigator	Customs inspector	Detective
Federal agent	Firefighter	Fire investigator

continued →

Government/Politics/Military (continued)

Fire safety inspector	Fish and game warden	Foreign service officer
Forensic scientist	Forest fire prevention specialist	Gambling surveillance officer
Health and safety specialist	Health information technician	Immigration attorney
Information security analyst	Intellectual property lawyer	Intelligence analyst
IRS agent	Judge	Judicial law clerk
Jury consultant	Legislator	Litigation support
Magistrate judge	Manager	Mediator
Military officer	Paralegal	Policy analyst
Political campaign staff	Political consultant	Political researcher
Politician	Protective service worker	Public interest advocate
Public interest lawyer	Statistician	Supervisor

Virtually every job title can be found within government work. Whether you are an attorney or a teacher, you can be hired by either a local, state, or federal government. So the titles here represent a small fraction of the possible jobs, and tend to focus on titles that are most often found within a government setting. If you have identified a specific career you'd like to pursue, always check to see if a government position might be available.

Health Care/Medical/Pharmaceutical

Anesthesiologist	Audiologist	Cardiologist
Cardiovascular technologist	Chiropractor	Clinical lab technician
Compliance specialist	Dentist	Diagnostic medical sonographer
Dietician	Drug developer	Emergency medical technician
Exercise physiologist	Genetic counselor	Health information technician
Hearing aid specialist	Home health aide	Massage therapist
Medical laboratory technician	Medical records specialist	Medical registrar
Medical transcriptionist	MRI technologist	Network security administrator

Health Care/Medical/Pharmaceutical (continued)

Network security engineer	Neurologist	Nuclear medicine technologist
Nurse	Nurse anesthetist	Nurse midwife
Nurse practitioner	Nursing assistant	Nutritionist
Obstetrician	Occupational health and safety specialist	Occupational therapist
Optician	Optometrist	Oral surgeon
Orthodontist	Orthotist/prosthetist	Paramedic
Pathologist	Personal care aide	Pharmacist
Pharmacy technician	Physical therapist	Physical therapist aide
Physician	Physician assistant	Podiatrist
Psychiatric technician	Public health specialist	Radiation therapist
Radiologist	Recreational therapist	Registered nurse
Respiratory therapist	Speech-language pathologist	Surgeon

Law/Security/Emergency Services

Administrative adjudicator	Administrative law judge	Administrator hearing officer
Animal control worker	Arbitrator	Attorney
Bailiff	Correctional officer	Court reporter
Criminal investigator	Cyber crime investigator	Detective
Emergency medical tech	Federal agent	Firefighter
Fire investigator	Forensic scientist	Forest fire inspector
Forest fire prevention specialist	Gambling surveillance officer	Health information technician
Immigration attorney	Information security analyst	Judge
Judicial law clerk	Jury consultant	Legal assistant
Legislator	Litigation support	Magistrate judge
Malware analyst	Mediator	Paralegal
Police officer	Prison administrator	Private investigator
Protective service worker	Security guard	Sheriff
State police	Transit and railroad police	Transportation security screener

Nonprofit/NGO

The nonprofit area involves virtually every job title you would find in the other areas. Nonprofit work is better defined by the type of organization for which you would work. Many nonprofit employers are categorized according to their mission or purpose. Examples of the areas in which nonprofit organizations can be categorized include:

- Arts, culture, and humanities
- Education and research
- Environment and animals
- Health
- Human services
- International
- Public or societal benefit
- Religion

If you're considering nonprofit work, focus first on the type of work you would like to do, and then find nonprofit organizations that focus on your area of interest. You can then seek out potential employers who can use your skills and knowledge.

Performing Arts/Entertainment

Actor	Agent	Animator
Announcer	Art director	Audio and video technician
Broadcast and sound engineering technician	Broadcast announcer	Broadcast technician
Camera operator	Choreographer	Comedian
Composer	Dancer	Director
Drama Coach	Film and video editor	Film director
Film producer	Lighting technician	Makeup artist
Music director	Musical theatre performer	Musician
Photographer	Podcast developer	Producer
Screenwriter	Set and exhibit designer	Singer
Sound engineering technician	Special effects artist	Talent scout
Theater director	Theater manager	Writer

Science/Research/Technology

Analytical chemist	Anthropologist	Archaeologist
Astronomer	Atmospheric and space scientist	Biochemist
Bioinformatics scientist	Biologist	Biophysicist
Botanist	Chemist	Epidemiologist
Food scientist	Forensic science technician	Forest and conservation technician
Forester	Geneticist	Geographer
Geologist	Geoscientist	Hydrologist
Life scientist	Marine biologist	Materials scientist
Mathematician	Medical research scientist	Microbiologist
Nanotechnologist	Neuroscientist	Nuclear technician
Occupational health and safety specialist	Oceanographer	Physical scientist
Physicist	Research and development manager	Research psychologist
Social science research assistant	Soil and plant scientist	Statistician

Sports/Leisure/Tourism

Athletic director	Athletic trainer	Chef
Corporate travel consultant	Cruise director	Event and conference organizer
Exercise physiologist	Expedition leader	Facility manager
Fitness instructor	Flight attendant	Food and beverage manager
Health and fitness director	Hotel manager	Instructor
Manufacturer's representative	Outdoor recreation planner	Professional athlete
Radio sports producer	Recreation manager	Recreation therapist
Spa manager	Sporting goods store manager	Sports and fitness nutritionist
Sportcaster	Sports events coordinator	Sports information director

continued →

Sports/Leisure/Tourism (continued)

Sports venue manager	Sportswriter	Stadium manager
Talent scout	Television sports producer	Tour and travel guide
Travel agent	Travel office manager	Youth program director

Knowing the predominant industry for your career interests will help you identify potential employers and alternate careers you might not have considered. For instance, if you indicated you were interested in being an athletic coach, you will note that there are a lot of sports-related careers under the Sports/Leisure/Tourism category, and there are also some under Education/Social Services/Psychological Services. You now have two major industries you could investigate to get more ideas.

Take note of the patterns you uncovered from the job title and meta-industry lists.

- Did you seem to select careers in one or two industries?
- Or are you choosing careers that could fit into a number of industries?
- Did one or more industry appeal in particular?
- Or are you all over the map?
- Do your selections seem more random than meaningful?

If you're all over the map, look through your list and see if you can find some commonalities among the careers you selected. For instance, maybe all the careers you selected are high-paying professions such as the law or medicine. Maybe you selected careers that tend to focus on interacting with people. Or maybe you lean toward careers where you're working with equipment or technology. Maybe you tend to select careers that require a graduate degree. You might have selected creative careers, regardless of the field they were in.

Doing this exercise can help open a new world of opportunities for you. Just knowing the general industry for your interests (if you tended to focus on an industry) or the characteristics of careers that interest you can help you find other opportunities related to what you initially considered. This list can be particularly helpful if the doors close on one career field for some reason. Every profession has related careers, many of which require less or different education. For instance, in the medical field, the careers that require the most education are physician and medical researcher. But if you like the field of medicine, your career choices are virtually unlimited from medical technician to physician's assistant. You don't need to limit yourself only to one job title within an industry.

To finish up this exercise:

- Write down the key industry or industries you are most interested in.
- Write down the job titles you want to start investigating.
- Put a star next to the top three you'd like to explore.
- Follow the chart on page 128 to determine your next step.

Evaluating What You Have Learned So Far

So now that you've made some preliminary decisions about possible career fields, take a few minutes to assess your choices. If you have more than one choice (recommended), do a compare and contrast of your responses using the prompts below. As you keep learning, this chart is an easy way to rate where you are with any field you're considering.

My knowledge level of this field	Low	Medium	High
Relationship of this field to my interests	Low	Medium	High
Relationship of this field to my knowledge	Low	Medium	High
Relationship of this field to my skills	Low	Medium	High
My willingness to do the necessary work to attain a job in this field	Low	Medium	High

This chart can be a great way to determine your next goals for the search. How could you learn more about your new choice? Through conversations with people? More internet research? An internship? How will you explore what's next?

Before we leave this chapter, it's important to take a moment to consider what happens when you encounter roadblocks in the process. What seems like a simple choice might not be so simple when other aspects of your life interfere, or when a choice you've wanted your whole life suddenly isn't an option anymore.

Think Like An Employer

When you are searching for a job, it's like you are on one long audition. Whether you are submitting your resume, being interviewed, or working as an intern, you are constantly being watched to see if you are the right actor for the part, so to speak. And you never know who might be noticing you. Keeping this in mind can be one of your personal secrets to success, because most people don't think this way. If you are thinking like this, then you are thinking like an employer, which is a smart thing to do. When faced with many candidates, employers have to choose. And you want to be their first choice. So consider these situations where you have a chance to be the best candidate.

If an employer is selecting candidates from resumes, will they choose:

- A perfectly written resume—or one with misspellings and poor formatting?
- A resume that is targeted to their position or industry—or a general resume that doesn't point to any particular job title or career?

When looking for candidates online, would an employer prefer:

- The candidate who has no social media presence—or the candidate who has a well-written LinkedIn account and an Instagram feed with lots of interesting activities related to the job search?

When interviewing a candidate on site, would an employer prefer:

- An interviewee who arrives ten minutes late, out of breath, having gotten lost on the way to the interview? Or the interviewee who shows up ten minutes early and uses the spare time to relax, breathe, and become composed?

When observing an intern at the organization, would an employer be more likely to retain:

- The intern who wanders aimlessly around looking for a place to work and "something to do"? Or the intern who checks in with supervisors, finds a valuable task, and gets to work at the nearest available table or flat surface?

When a Choice Doesn't Work— or There Is No Choice

Although I use the word "choice," sometimes it doesn't feel like you have a choice. Your choice might have been to go to medical school, but you didn't get accepted. Or your choice might have been to get a job with a high-powered consulting firm, but your GPA prevented being considered. The economy might be great when you graduate or it could be terrible. So, in the one sense, you didn't have a choice. Not with those variables. But what you need to do now is look at what your new choices are. What are the options still available to you? It can feel like you don't have options when your "dream" has been taken away, but here again I caution you not to be a fortune-teller. There are way too many stories about people who thought they had hit the lowest point in their lives only to have an amazing opportunity show up, an opportunity they wouldn't have seen if they had pursued their first dream.

We always have a choice. We have a choice of how to view any situation. So err on the side of being positive. Err on the side of assuming something else will appear for you.

Psychological Traps

Choosing a career seems like it should be easy and logical. Remember the diagram, on page 102, about the process of making a choice and then learning and then making other choices? Logical, right? You look at the lists of careers and you make some choices, learn about them, and then make your selection of which career to pursue. However, what makes this process seem so simple on the surface is the lack of negative judgment. But judgment is all around, unfortunately. Your own mind (and family and friends and even strangers) will want to offer opinions of everything you're doing, and sometimes those opinions are helpful and sometimes they're not. So let's pause and look at some mental components that can complicate the decision-making process and how you can overcome them.

1 **Overwhelming yourself.** Thinking you must know all the career options before you can choose will be overwhelming. After all, the *Dictionary of Occupational Titles* lists more than 13,000 job titles. You will never fully know all the jobs and opportunities that are out there. And you don't have to. You don't need to. That's why this book started with *you*, not the job market. When you were completing the

various exercises in the first part of this book, you likely eliminated majors and interest areas that weren't appealing to you. That's what you will also do in the job market. Start by eliminating what doesn't interest you.

2 **Fortune-telling.** Playing fortune-teller and trying to predict everything will just stress you out. You might be able to predict some general ideas ("I think I'd like to work in a hospital setting"), but it's okay to stay open to what your specific job might be in the future. If your mind insists on fortune-telling, focus on the most positive ways to think about something. Predict the good things that will happen.

3 **Fear and anxiety.** Everyone feels anxious in this process. It's normal. Just don't let it hold you back. Remind yourself that you're making some big decisions, so it's okay to feel unsure or worried. Just don't stop. Keep moving forward, and the more you move forward, the more you practice your interviewing skills, the less your anxiety will overwhelm you.

4 **Rigid thinking.** If you are stuck with how things should be, you won't be open to new solutions or ideas. Focus your energies on being curious. Keeping a curious mindset will help you stay open to possibilities. You will then want to do the necessary research to learn more about what you want to do. A curious person is seldom bored, tired, or depressed. Curiosity creates its own energy.

Now What?

You've done all the exercises. And you have some ideas at this point. For some of you, those ideas are not just ideas but fully fleshed out goals, and you're ready to move forward. For others, they are still ideas, and you're ready to explore them further before making a commitment. Regardless, you're ready to tackle the rest of this book and keep using the Parachute System. So let's do one more look at where you are and where you can go next.

Think of the career field or title you're considering. After you've made your choice, ask yourself, "Can I do this tomorrow?" Take a look at the chart on the facing page and develop your plan, based on your response to that simple question.

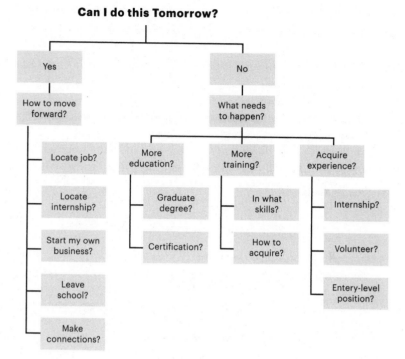

Can I do this Tomorrow?

Do you see how asking this one simple question, "Can I do it tomorrow?" helps you develop a plan for what to do next in your process. Now, once again, the questions are simple, but the process requires thinking.

Where Are You Landing?

Let's go back to that original metaphor of the irrigation circles providing landing spots for your parachute jump. Now that you've identified your fields of interest, where do you hope to land? What's the next step in your process? As you consider these questions, here are some basic possibilities,

- **A traditional job.** This would be where someone or some organization gives you a paycheck. It could be in a traditional setting, such as a bank or a hospital or a school, or it could be in an entrepreneurial setting, like a start-up or a new venture, but the bottom line is you are receiving a paycheck from an outside entity. (See chapter 9 for more information.)

- **An internship, gap experience, or other short-term experience.** In this setting you are still very much a learner, and learning is your primary goal. You may or may not be paid, depending on the field. You are in this mostly to learn, to make new contacts, and, hopefully, find a mentor or two. (See chapter 10 for more guidance.)

- **Your own business.** You are the boss, so to speak, and the pay you receive comes from your work. You might be funded by venture capitalists or through a grant. What's most important here is to seek outside help. Find someone to mentor you. You don't know what you don't know, and new businesses are fraught with potential problems. That's why only about 50 percent of new businesses succeed in the first five years. You also might not be aware of legal restrictions or implication about your areas of interest, so it pays to do your homework if this is your plan for the future.

- **Graduate or professional school.** If through your explorations you have learned that the only way to move ahead in your desired profession (medicine, law, college professor) is to acquire additional education, then that may be your next step after college. But be sure you have researched this carefully. Sometimes students assume they must get another degree, when it's not necessary. For instance, if you're going into business, there are plenty of jobs that don't require an MBA. And many of the best MBA programs would prefer that you have experience before you enroll, so you are likely better off pursuing work before a degree in that field. However, if you know you want to be a lawyer, you might as well go to law school. Just make sure you have thoroughly checked out the profession through internships, shadowing experiences, conversations with actual lawyers, and conversations with law students. (See chapter 11 for more in-depth thinking about this.)

  Before you leave this section of the chapter, try listing:

THE INDUSTRY(IES) THAT FIT YOU	THE CAREER FIELDS WITHIN THAT INDUSTRY THAT FIT YOU	SPECIFIC JOB TITLES THAT FIT YOU	WHAT DO YOU NEED TO DO NOW?

CHAPTER 6

Create Your Resume

Seriously, resumes? Is this chapter even needed? Aren't resumes so twentieth century?

Books and articles have been announcing the death of the resume for more than twenty years, but you know what? You still need one. Not always, and not in every job search context, but you will find it necessary at several points in your job-search process. Here are just a few places where a resume will come in handy:

- If you're using on-campus recruiting. Most employers use resumes to screen applicants.
- If you're applying for a job online. Most sites ask you to upload a resume.
- If you've been offered a job through a connection. The human resources office still wants your resume for their files.
- On a graduate or professional school application. Sometimes they will call it a "vita."
- At a job or internship fair.
- At a networking event.

- Anywhere with limited social media access or where your LinkedIn profile is inaccessible.
- Whenever anyone who can help you asks for it.

Does that give you enough incentive to start writing this document that almost everyone dreads? (Even I, as an experienced career counselor and coach, waited to write this chapter until the end!)

If you still need some motivation to get started, resumes are good for more than your job search. They can also be a great way to keep track of all your accomplishments and activities over the years. That's why updating your resume at least once a semester is a great idea. Use your resume to summarize your education and experiences, help you focus on key accomplishments, and provide potential talking points and stories for your interviews.

A common reason students cite for not writing a resume is the theory that LinkedIn has replaced resumes. And in some ways it has. Often an employer will look you up on LinkedIn before reviewing any other materials about you. It's a quick and easy way to learn about your skills and experiences. However, unless you plan to open your laptop at an interview, a printed resume is still one of best ways to communicate the breadth of your experience in person. And since print medium is different from online, a resume provides a different reader experience from LinkedIn.

In this chapter, we'll focus on the key things you need to keep in mind when you write your resume.

- Everybody has an opinion about resumes.
- Generally, these opinions conflict with one another.
- Listen to all the advice and then create the resume you think sells you the best.
- Play by the rules unless you have an incredible reason not to.
- Don't write it alone. Get someone to help you. Preferably someone who knows resumes well, like someone in your career center or in human resources.

Resume Templates

Let's talk about templates. You will find tons of resume formats and samples online—everywhere from your own career center's webpage to your Microsoft Word or Google doc programs. (Don't believe me? Just Google "resume templates" and let the fun begin.)

Let me make this easy for you: use the templates when they are helpful. If you find a template or style that fits you and fits the field you're interested in (more on that in a minute), download the template and try it out. If you find it isn't working for you, or it's too hard to fit your experience into the structure, then that's not the right template.

As mentioned, there are a million places online to find resume templates. Unfortunately, a lot of them are bad. Or not designed for the career field you're seeking a job in. So here are some tips as you search for templates.

- Start with your career center's website. Most career centers create their own sample student resumes, and they tend to base them on what has succeeded for previous students. They also know what the employers are typically seeking in a resume. Your career center might even subscribe to resume-writing software.

- Keep your formatting straightforward and easy to read.

- Content wins over style. You can have the most attractive resume but if the content is lacking, it won't work. And the employer must be able to scan and find the content they are seeking in a few seconds. Unusual or creative formats often make the employer search too hard.

- Many larger employers use some form of artificial intelligence to scan resumes. And strange formats (lots of underlining or italics, for example) can make it hard for the scanner to read.

- Stay away from the artsy resumes online, the ones with weird formatting and information placed all over in little boxes, the ones with pictures, or unusual fonts, or emojis, or other "cute" ideas. You don't want cute even if you're applying to work with five-year-olds. You are the professional—remember that. Let the five-year-olds be cute.

At this point in any presentation I give about resume-writing, the following question pops up:

"But what if I'm going into a creative field, like advertising or marketing? Shouldn't I have a creative and unique resume that sells my skills?"

Maybe. You can also have a traditional resume and demonstrate your creativity through your portfolio of sample works, or through your LinkedIn or other social media profiles. Creative resumes do work with some people. There will always be the success story of someone who printed their resume on orange paper to appeal to a University of Tennessee employer, but there are many more failures that aren't reported, because who's going to report about their failed orange resume?

One final note about searching for online templates: Be careful about companies that offer to write your resume for a fee. Some are quite legitimate and perfectly fine, but do your research before you pay someone else for your resume. You really can do it yourself. And that's better, because it's a document that represents your life. To ask someone else to write it is like asking someone else to write your memoir. Sure, they could do that, but they will never have your voice, and they won't be able to explain things the way you would. So take some time to write your resume. Use your career center for help.

The Ten Rules of Resume-Writing

Well, these are really guidelines, but break them at your own risk.

1 Proofread. Failure to proofread and catch errors is the easiest reason to reject a resume. So ask others to proofread. And then proofread again. Proofread for:

- Misspelled words
- Poor grammar
- Unclear content or abbreviations
- Mismatched subjects/verbs
- Mixed past/present tense
- Misaligned or inconsistent formatting. (If you use periods at the ends of some bullet points, use them with all. If you italicize one job title, italicize them all.)
- Lack of keywords
- Poor bullet point construction
- The words "I," "responsible for," or "duties included," which should be eliminated
- Too many bold or italicized words, making the resume hard to read
- Anything else that might distract the reader from your wonderful background.

2 Target your resume to the position and career field you're seeking. It's better to send out ten targeted resumes than one hundred generic ones. You target your resume by using keywords, action verbs, and competencies. More on that later.

3 No need to list each of your classes unless you are highlighting something unique. (For example, no need to list microeconomics if you're an economics major. That course is assumed. But if you took Basic coding that would be unique and worth listing.)

4 Focus on accomplishments through facts, numbers, and quick explanations. Use your cover letter for longer explanations or stories.

5 Make sure everyone will understand your job descriptions. Write clear bullet points that clearly explain what you did.

6 Once you're a junior, remove high school information unless immediately relevant (you attended a prep school and are seeking a teaching position there). The assumption at this point is you did well enough in high school to enter your college—it's time to show off what you have been doing in college.

7 Employers will assume you know Word, Excel, Outlook, or the Google equivalent. Those entries won't enhance your computer skills section.

8 Most college students can keep their resumes to one page, and this is recommended. Some employers or uploading sites won't take a resume that's longer than one page. You can create an alternate resume that's longer and share that in an interview, or post it on LinkedIn.

9 Don't bother with foreign languages unless you are fluent, or some knowledge is necessary for the job.

10 Always convert your resume to a PDF before sending it in an email or posting online. And double-check the PDF before you send it. Sometimes line errors in your Word doc will show up on a PDF. Your one-page resume may suddenly have one line on a second page. You might have to go back to the original to correct the problem.

Making Your Resume Stand Out from the Pack: Bullet Points

You know that content rules in a resume, so how can you make sure your content attracts the right employers? By writing bullet point entries that are relevant to the position, using keywords that fit what the employer is seeking.

- Use bullet points to highlight soft skills, specific job-related skills, and competencies.

- Bullet points should always be targeted to the position you are seeking; so if you're seeking different positions, you will need to adjust them.

Let's take a typical resume entry, "Provided customer service." That's something many of you have done, whether you have worked in a coffee shop, staffed a front desk at an office, or worked in a store. Most people will know what that phrase means—but what does it mean to you? Take a few minutes and recall the times you had to "provide customer service" (or whatever phrase works for your experience). Ask yourself questions to get at the details of the experience. What made your experience unique or better?

Here is a before-and-after example for a waitress position, for someone who wants to move into a consulting firm.

ORIGINAL BULLET POINT	CLARIFYING QUESTIONS	REVISED BULLET POINTS
• Provided customer service • Waited on and cleared tables • Processed payments	• To whom? • Under what conditions? Busy, stressful? • Demanding customers? High level of expertise needed? • Were you better at it? Were you recognized or complimented?	• Quickly and efficiently handled more than 100 customers during busy lunch hour and ensured customer satisfaction through constant communication and follow-through • Received minimum 20 percent tips for 98 percent of orders with customers specifically requesting my tables

Do you see how she was able to transform a traditional waitress role into an example of pleasing clients? She used her strong tips and the fact that customers chose her tables as proof that she did her job well. If she can please clients in her waitress role through clear communication and efficiency, she can do the same with the consulting clients. She also has the basis for a great interview story.

Try using this same approach with your bullet points. And check out the next section on keywords, so you can use them to enhance your bullet point statements.

Making Your Resume Stand Out from the Pack: Keywords, Action Verbs, and Competencies

Bullet points aren't the only way to make your resume stand out. The words you choose to describe your experiences and education can cause an employer to put your resume at the top of the stack. Using keywords, action verbs, and competencies is a powerful trick for getting attention. Let's examine these techniques further.

KEYWORDS

Keywords are a secret weapon and one of the most powerful tools you have for writing a targeted resume designed to appeal to a particular employer or industry.

You can use keywords throughout your resume, from the (optional) skills section to the education and experience sections. When you describe your experience in bullet points, for example, try to use at least two or three keywords relevant to the position you're seeking.

One of the best places to find keywords for your resume is in the job description for the position you're applying to. Look through the description and note the words used. Include those same words in your resume. You can also Google "keywords for _____ positions" and see what words show up. Which ones can you legitimately use in your resume to make it clear you understand the lingo of a profession?

Every field has its own keywords. If you've already worked in a field, you may know them. Do an online search for keywords related to your field. Take a look at your experiences and education and jot down the ones that you can reasonably use. Honesty is imperative here: do not list keywords that imply you know something you don't. If you're going into accounting and you learn that "stockholder reporting" is a keyword, but you've never had anything to do with that, don't just add it to your skills.

ACTION VERBS

Action verbs can keep you from using the dreaded "responsible for" or "duties included" phrases that tank your resume.

Action verbs can be another form of relevant keywords. If you're seeking a position in sales and you are currently a resident advisor, think about times when you had to use some sort of sales skill. What about the many times you had to round up students to attend programs on your floor? Consider how reluctant they were, and how you enticed them with food. Well, that experience has lots of sales-related action verb potential: "influenced," "marketed," "advertised," "promoted," "increased attendance by ____ %," "publicized," "designed," and so on.

In the table that follows, there are some generic action verbs that would interest employers.

SAMPLE ACTION VERBS

Administered	Analyzed	Authored	Budgeted	Calculated
Coded	Communicated	Connected	Contributed	Coordinated
Created	Delivered	Designed	Developed	Established
Facilitated	Founded	Increased	Led	Managed
Negotiated	Performed	Produced	Strengthened	Trained

What actions or activities are associated with your proposed career field?

What action verbs would you want to include in your resume? If you are going into a health care field, for instance, you might want to use words such as advocated, aided, assessed, counseled, diagnosed, documented, evaluated, helped, or referred. Knowing the correct action verbs to use can greatly improve your chances of being selected for an interview.

COMPETENCIES

Remember in chapter 3 when we were examining your skills? We also discussed what are called "competencies," and if you look back on page 58 you'll see a list of the many competencies employers are seeking. Hopefully you filled out that list and indicated what your competencies are. If so, how might you use those competencies on your resume?

Components of a Resume

Now that you understand the value of action verbs, keywords, and competencies in creating a targeted resume that will entice an employer, let's break down the components of a resume.

HEADING

In the heading you traditionally put your name, address, email, and cell phone. You can put your name in a slightly larger font than the rest of the text, although generally not more than two sizes up. For example, if your resume is printed in a 12-point font, your name can be in a 14-or 16-point font.

These days, you might want to eliminate your street address. You can put the city and state where you live if you want, but because your resume may be posted on LinkedIn or other public sites, it's best not to have your home address for security reasons. Consider adding your LinkedIn profile address to your heading. (Just make sure that your resume and LinkedIn profile agree on the facts—an employer will be suspicious if you have different dates or different employers on your resume versus your LinkedIn account.)

Here's a typical heading:

Maya Williams

San Bernardino, CA | (111) 555–1212
mayatwilliams@myemail.edu | linkedin.com/MayaWilliams

Now that you've finished your heading, you have a choice. You can choose a summary, skills, education, or an experience section.

SUMMARY SECTION (OPTIONAL)

The summary section is essentially the written version of your elevator pitch. You might say something like "History major with three years of progressive leadership experience, strong background in research, and excellent writing skills."

The question is: does this add to your profile and your resume? It might, if the employer is seeking someone with leadership, research, and writing skills. But, hopefully, the experience you have will sell you without the need for a summary section. Summary sections tend to be more valuable when you have extensive experience and are trying to encapsulate it into a short statement. Evaluate for yourself whether it's necessary. And whatever you do, avoid fluffy statements that don't mean anything, like "successfully strive for perfection in all I do."

SKILLS SECTION (OPTIONAL)

One way to call an employer's attention to your skills is to create a skills section. You can use this section to highlight special skills or talents, such as computer programming languages, software skills, social media skills, or other special talents that might appeal to an employer.

But be careful: you should know that employers don't necessarily trust what candidates say about their skills. Many candidates list so many skills it's hard to believe they excel at all of them. Such skill lists then become meaningless. So only list the skills for which you can tell a good story to an employer and demonstrate the times you have used it successfully. Select two or three key skills that are most relevant. Here are some sample key skills with enough information to back them up as legitimate.

SKILLS

- **Leadership:** Three years managing student organization, doubling membership and revenue.
- **Programming:** Created an app to identify student volunteers, adopted by student affairs department.
- **Entrepreneurship:** Created business plan resulting in $50,000 angel investment.

EDUCATION SECTION

The next section is either your education section (if you're still a student, recent grad, and you want to highlight your education) or your experience section (if you've graduated, or your work experience is more compelling than your education). Always consider what will sell you to the employer—is it your education and the name of your school, or is it your experience?

- Use reverse chronological order, with the most recent degree first.
- If you financed your degree, you can include that as well.

You should think about potential keywords for this section. Your college can serve as a keyword, so if you attended more than one, list them all. You can also list specific courses if their title or keyword would interest an employer. Your choice. In this situation, we'll start with your education section.

You can add "relevant coursework" or "additional coursework," if
you've taken courses outside your major that would be relevant to an
employer. Don't list courses that would normally be part of a major.

EXPERIENCE SECTION

The experience section is arguably the most important part of your
resume. The best way to demonstrate that you are capable of succeeding
in a job is to demonstrate where you have succeeded in similar situations in the past. Your experience section creates the opportunity for
you to describe your previous experiences in terms of the position you
hope to get. Read through the following bullet points to strengthen
your presentation of your experiences. Be sure you incorporate the
guidance given in the previous sections of the resume.

This is one example of a format you could use to describe your
experience:

Name of company/organization, City, State, dates employed
Job title in italics
One or two line description of your overall responsibilities and type
of work that you did. (This is optional; you can just move directly into
the bullet points.)

- Three to five bullet points to highlight key accomplishments, using
  active verbs.
- Experiences listed in reverse chronological order (meaning start
  with your most recent experience and go backward).

- Focus on the most relevant experiences. (You don't have to list every job you've ever had.)
- Use standard fonts like Arial, Times New Roman, or Calibri in 10 to 12 point.
- Experience is experience, whether you were paid or not. So don't hesitate to list volunteer experiences, part-time positions, and internships.
- Do not add supervisor names, salaries, or reasons for leaving.
- Use the first person form of the verb, when using present tense to describe a current role. For instance, if you compile and analyze data in your role, list it as "Compile and analyze data for" . . . not "Compiles and analyzes data" . . . as if you're writing about someone else. (This is a common mistake when people use their job description to populate their resume.)

One way to analyze an experience is to ask yourself:

1 What did I do on this job? What did I create? What did I accomplish?
2 How did I do this? What methods did I use to achieve my goals?
3 What was the result of achieving those goals or doing a particular task?
4 How can I best explain this? What terminology should I use?

Keep in mind that you can create two (sometimes three) experience sections. This is particularly helpful when your most recent job doesn't relate to the career you are seeking, although an earlier position does. For instance, you are seeking a job in the finance field and last summer you worked in a bank, but right now you're working as a bartender while in school. If you follow strict chronological guidelines, your bartender job would have to be at the top of your experience section. So how do you get around this? You create a "Finance/Banking Experience" section and place all finance- and banking-related experiences (your summer job at the bank, your treasurer role in an organization, and the special finance seminar you took for four weeks one summer) in this section. Then you have another section called "Customer Service Experience" or "Additional Experience" where you can list your current bartending job.

You can leave the bartending job off completely, if you want, but it never hurts to demonstrate how hard-working you are, and supporting yourself while in school is a strength that impresses many employers.

Some students choose to separate "Leadership" from "Experience," but many times a leadership experience can take as much time and require as many skills as a job. If what you have accomplished is meaningful and professional, consider including a leadership experience within your overall experience section.

INTERESTS SECTION (OPTIONAL)

This section is mildly controversial, with some employers believing it is a waste of space and others who enjoy seeing a person's interests. If you have interesting hobbies, go for it. You never know when your hobby might entice someone. Otherwise, if you're pressed for space or your hobbies aren't that interesting, let it go.

It's Time to Start Writing Your Resume if You Haven't Already

If you have completed the exercises in chapters 2 to 4, then you should be ready to write a basic resume. You can target the resume when you determine where you will be sending it.

- Research the industry you hope to work in before you create your resume. Know what typical skills are needed for the positions and what the most common duties are.
- Use keywords. Know trends in the field.
- Create a basic outline based on templates and the guidelines presented in this chapter and then take it to your career center for review.

It's a good idea to have a master resume that contains everything you've done, and then reduce it to one page by selecting only the most relevant entries to apply for a specific position.

A sample template for a traditional resume is shown on page 142.

Name

City, State | Email | Phone | LinkedIn

EDUCATION

University Name / City, State   Month, Year
Bachelor of Arts/Science, Name of Major — GPA: 3.XX
Minor or concentration
Relevant coursework

Study Abroad University Name / City, State   Month, Year
(Explanation of program: foreign language, lived with family,
coursework—if relevant to plans. Otherwise just indicate the
university, location, and dates.)

Previous college or university / City, State   Month, Year
(if you are a transfer student)

High school / City, State   Month, Year
(if you are still a freshman or sophomore, or if relevant)

EXPERIENCE (Label this as is or target specific subsets of your experiences)

Organization Name / City, State   Month, Year
Title (If intern, use a description, e.g., "marketing intern")
Write a few sentences describing overall position and duties if desired.
- Bullet point 1 that highlights a key accomplishment.
- Bullet point 2 that highlights a key accomplishment.
- Bullet point 3 that highlights a key accomplishment.

LEADERSHIP EXPERIENCE
(Optional, but useful if employer indicates an interest in leadership skills)

Student Organization Name / City, State   Month, Year
President (date), Vice-President (date), Treasurer (date)
- Bullet point 1 that highlights a key accomplishment.
- Bullet point 2 that highlights a key accomplishment.
- Bullet point 3 that highlights a key accomplishment.

SKILLS or INTERESTS (Optional—use if relevant or enhances your image)

Language: (Include if conversational, fluent, read/write,
native in any language other than English)

Technical: (For computer software and programming languages,
include proficiency and familiarity)

Science/research: (Use if appropriate)

Interests: (List interesting activities you enjoy that might
be helpful in interviews and conversations)

RESUME RUBRIC FOR JOB SEEKERS

As a final check go through your resume and note the items you want to change to make yours fit into the "competitive" column in the following rubric. You might want to share your resume and this rubric with a friend or someone at the career center and ask them to review your resume as well.

	COMPETITIVE	SATISFACTORY	NEEDS IMPROVEMENT
Format and Overall Content	• Fills the page • Not overcrowded or sparse • Consistent font size and type, bolding, and section titles • No spelling or grammatical errors • Appropriate length for position and years of experience • Name and contact information clear and complete • Sections are ordered in optimal fashion • Content within sections is in reverse chronological order	• Fills one page • Consistent font size and type, bolding, and section titles • No spelling or grammatical errors • Name and contact information clear and complete • Experiences generally in reverse chronological order	• Inappropriate length for position: too short or too long • Difficult to read • Inconsistent font size and type, bolding, and section titles • Multiple spelling or grammatical errors • Fails to include contact info or email name is unprofessional • Inconsistent presentation of information • Order of sections is not ideal • Not in reverse chronological order

continued →

Resume Rubric for Job Seekers (continued)

	COMPETITIVE	SATISFACTORY	NEEDS IMPROVEMENT
Experience Section	• Title, organization, where and when worked presented consistently • Uses strong action verbs • Descriptions highlight skills and accomplishments clearly, concisely, and effectively • Skills relevant to position sought • Uses keywords relevant to employer	• Uses some action verbs • Descriptions highlight experience but not clearly or concisely • Descriptions don't always consider relevance to employer • Mixes use of active and passive voice	• Title, organization, where and when worked not presented consistently • Does not use action verbs • Uses "responsible for" • Descriptions do not highlight skills • Does not describe skills or accomplishments • No keywords • Presents information not relevant to employer
Education Section	• Lists degrees received, dates, name of institution(s), and GPA (if 3.0 or better) • Describes relevant coursework • Describes relevant experiences, including internships, honors, and study abroad • Presents information in a consistent and easy-to-read manner	• Lists degrees received, name of institution(s), and GPA (if 3.0 or better)	• Does not list degree or graduation date • Fails to include additional training or other relevant education • Presents information inconsistently or otherwise difficult to understand

CHAPTER 7

Start Conversations

LinkedIn, Social Media, and Cover Letters

As you may have already noticed, your job search is a community experience. You will need the help and support of others to succeed. This can be a source of stress if you don't have a lot of family or personal connections. But that's the great benefit of social media. You don't have to have family connections: you can build your own.

Now that you have created a strong portrait of yourself and your talents, and perhaps even know where or how you want to apply your talents, it's time to let the world know about you. And by the world, we mean potential employers and people who can connect you to employers.

This chapter will focus on using your writing and social media skills to connect with potential employers. Social media can level the playing field for job seekers. Think of social media as a great way to start a conversation. You don't have to know a lot of people in your career area initially; you can build up your connections through social media. Whether you're a regular social media user or influencer, or whether you'd rather do anything besides look at an Instagram account, this chapter will help you make the most efficient use of your social media in the job search.

You might be wondering whether you could choose to not use social media and, of course, you can make that choice. But some surveys have shown that employers are actually a little suspicious when their candidates don't have anything posted. Having at least one social media account (and for most job seekers, I recommend LinkedIn) will help an employer see your skills. Plus why wouldn't you want to use one of the most powerful tools you have in the job search? You won't likely get a job through social media, but social media will connect you to people, and those people will connect you to the job.

Bottom line: it's better to have a social media profile than not. Social media gives you such a visible platform to share your stories and demonstrate your skills, so why not? But it is easy to get overwhelmed by all the options, so use this chapter to determine the best social media platforms for the career field you're seeking.

The Value of Keywords—Again

In chapter 6 you explored keyword usage related to your resume. Well, don't put away your keywords—you will need them for your social media and for cover letters. Keywords are a great way to efficiently search through the tons of job listings you will find on social media. They are also a great way to ensure that you are using the correct language that will attract employers to your online profiles. The increasing use of data analytics and artificial intelligence makes proper keyword use imperative. If the bot reading your email or online profile can't find the words it is seeking, it will move on, no matter how wonderful your experience is.

By using keywords in your social media, you appear more professional than the typical job seeker. You are telling the employer that you know the field and you know the terminology. Think if you were going to take a piano class and the instructor said those "black and white things" as opposed to "black and white keys." How much would you trust someone who didn't know that a piano has keys? Or if a guitar teacher talked about those "metal strips that go across the neck" as opposed to calling them frets. It might make you doubt their ability to teach you anything. It's the same way with career fields. Knowing the basic terminology automatically gives you some gravitas that other job seekers won't have.

As mentioned previously, a great place to find keywords is to simply select your industry and then Google "keywords for _____." As with your resume, keywords related to action verbs and competencies are important to include in your social media.

Sometimes a job title can be a great keyword, particularly if it is descriptive. That's why you don't want to simply list "intern" as your job title. You will want to list "marketing intern" or "financial consulting intern" instead. Words such as "financial," "consulting," and "marketing" are excellent keywords if you're considering those fields, no matter what specific industry you're seeking. For instance, marketing professionals are needed in virtually every employer sector—you have as much chance finding a nonprofit opportunity as a business opportunity with the word "marketing." Consultants exist in every industry as well.

A company name can be helpful as a keyword. If a recruiter is seeking someone with hospitality experience, for example, they might use "Disney" as a keyword, hoping to find people who work for or were trained by Disney.

Even the name of your college can be a keyword. Sometimes employers are seeking individuals from a particular school, or a particular major, so all of those terms can be useful as well. Alumni like to hire individuals who went to the same school, so it's not unusual for potential employers to start candidate searches by using their schools' names.

Your action verbs and competencies can be listed and demonstrated through your social media as well. Next let's take a look at using specific platforms (and guidelines for those platforms) to make connections.

Social Media Planning Guide for the Job Search

You don't have to be active on all social media platforms. At the time of this writing, the most popular platforms with job seekers are LinkedIn, Twitter, Facebook, Instagram, YouTube, and Pinterest. Other apps, like Snapchat, Groupme, and so on, are more likely to be local and not necessarily helpful for expanding your network. Below is a basic way to think about your social media usage for job hunting.

CONTENT: IN THIS SECTION, LIST THE BASIC CONTENT YOU PLAN TO PRODUCE OR HAVE PRODUCED.	AUDIENCE: PRESUMABLY EMPLOYERS, BUT WHO ELSE ARE YOU ATTRACTING?	KEY POINTS/ PURPOSE: WHY ARE YOU POSTING?
• Your resume is content—where will you post it? • Any videos you've produced • PowerPoint presentations • Photographs • Links to relevant research articles or current events • Your own writing	• Who will see this post? • What companies, organizations, or employers are you targeting? • How will you tailor your content to attract that audience? • What skills is your employer seeking?	• What are the key elements you want the reader to focus on? • What information do you want to share? • How might what you're posting impress someone? • What skills are you conveying?

POSTING/ PLATFORM: FAMILIARIZE YOURSELF WITH THE VARIOUS PLATFORMS.	ACTION PLAN: WHAT DO YOU NEED TO DO NEXT?
• Which social media platforms best fit the information you want to convey? • What are your plans for posting frequency? • What media will you be posting? Is it consistent with the platform?	• What are the steps to set up your accounts? • Do you have a consistent photo and name? • Do you have content ready to share? • Do you have the proper security settings for content you want the public to see versus private content?

Now that you have an idea of which platforms you might use, let's review some basic guidelines. The truth is, by the time this book is printed, there will likely be a new hot social media platform, but the same general rules will apply.

General Guidelines for All Social Media Use

1 For any of these platforms, the best way to get started is to visit the website and watch any tutorials posted. You can also check YouTube for instructions. Read through any guidelines or information provided and set up an account. Don't purchase paid subscriptions initially if a free option is available. This will give you a chance to see if the site is useful and whether you need to spend any money on it.

2 Always read any privacy guidelines or security protections for the site. In general, until you're ready to show your site to the public, keep it private. You can open it up later. Check all the privacy settings and the notification settings so you're not sharing too much with others or receiving too many emails from the site.

3 Review the profiles of others to see how they present themselves and interact with others.

4 Fill out your profile as fully as possible. Your profile is one of the first things an employer will read, so keep keywords in mind, as well as the need to be professional. Always link to other social media sites you have developed. For instance, you can link to your Twitter account from your LinkedIn account.

5 Have a professional picture for your profile. Use the same picture on all sites if you want to start creating a brand or look. Check with your career center; they may offer to take your picture with a neutral background. Look for "LinkedIn Photo Booths" at career fairs and other events.

6 Always pick a professional name—it doesn't have to be your real name (except with LinkedIn), but it needs to be something that shows you're using this site for serious reasons. If your name is taken, try adding something neutral, like your zip code or a middle name, to differentiate yourself.

7 Look for your career center's social media presence and follow their account. Look for other college or university career center sites and follow them if they post interesting and helpful items. (If they are just advertising their own programs, they probably won't be helpful.)

8 Start following people whose posts interest you.

9 Follow professional associations, companies, organizations, and interest-related groups.

10 Write intelligent and interesting posts (or Pins) and share publicly. Humor and "cute" memes are fine occasionally, but if you're trying to impress an employer, don't do too much of that.

- If you find an interesting article related to your field, post it. Add some comments if you'd like to share your opinion or call the reader's attention to something.
- Review books or articles related to your field or on general business topics. Promote the ones you like. (No point in being negative online about a book. Just don't write about it.)
- Post something about your favorite writer or researcher of the month.
- Repost interesting items from companies you'd like to work for.
- Be sure to use hashtags or "@" to identify keywords or key individuals or companies.
- Look for popular hashtags that a potential employer might also use.

On the following page is a quick chart to help you identify and efficiently use the best social media for your career plans.

LinkedIn

- Fill out profile completely
- Keep it up-to-date
- Start developing connections
- Use LinkedIn.com/alumni link to find alumni
- Join alumni groups
- Follow groups by profession
- Search for jobs and internships
- Search companies by location and relevance to interests
- Follow companies of interest
- Turn off group notifications

Twitter

- Find key voices/influencers in your field
- Follow key experts
- Follow organizations
- Post interesting info and articles related to your career
- Use and search hashtags such as #recruiters, #humanresources, #jobs, #jobsearch, #EmployerName, #city where you'd like to live, #related to anything you're interested in, #Resume, #Hireme, etc.

Facebook

- See if your desired employer has a site
- Follow potential employers
- Post positive comments on the site
- Ask questions
- Join groups related to your career interests
- Participate in groups: ask questions, share advice; share a link to an article
- Guard your privacy settings

Instagram

- Follow companies or organizations
- Follow your career center or other university career centers
- Post pictures of your projects or accomplishments
- Use hashtags such as #nowhiring and #hiring
- Look up special groups such as "Bookstagram" for publishing and writing topics

Pinterest

- Search using keywords such as "resume" or "interviews"
- Create a board about your career field or job search
- Pin videos of interest to your career area
- Make sure your boards are visible
- Look for tips on interview clothing, resume samples, interview tips, and job information
- Follow users and organizations
- Follow career centers and career advisors
- Great for marketing, graphic designers, artists

YouTube

- Look up specific career topics such as: elevator pitches, behavioral interviewing, LinkedIn, best practices in the job search, creating a video resume, and so on
- Look up career experts who post lots of helpful videos such as Ted Talks
- Post your own videos if they are professional and related to your areas of interest

Creating Your LinkedIn Account

LinkedIn is arguably the best social media platform you can use for the job search. Although some careers related to academic and artistic fields don't use it as much, LinkedIn represents the largest professional social network online and it continues to grow. It represents the best way to be seen by potential employers, keep up with trends in your field, connect with key leaders and influencers—and even potentially become an influencer yourself. Through LinkedIn you will be able to develop a network, share your expertise, and connect with alumni from your high school or college. **If you only have time to create one social media account, LinkedIn is likely your best bet.**

But here's a warning: LinkedIn is used by many job seekers and people trying to sell their services, and not all of them have learned to use it properly. As a result, many professionals are jaded about connecting to people they don't know. They also don't want to be hit with that "I want to pick your brain" or "I need a job" request that can end up taking their time with no benefit. So when you do reach out, be respectful that you are taking someone else's time. Know why you are reaching out and state it. If you don't hear back, you can send a "nudge" to them, but that's it. Don't keep asking. Not everyone has the time or interest in connecting with the world at large, even if they are an alumnus of your institution. Never start by asking for a job or a favor. Start by connecting and then follow-up with a request when/if appropriate.

You can find a ton of information on how to set up and improve your LinkedIn account from LinkedIn itself. They offer a variety of tutorial videos and instructions on Lynda.com at https://www.lynda.com/LinkedIn-training-tutorials/473-0.html.

In addition, there are an assortment of excellent books on LinkedIn. Just keep in mind that due to publication delays, sometimes LinkedIn might make changes that aren't reflected in the book. One of the best LinkedIn resources is *LinkedIn Profile Optimization for Dummies* by Donna Serdula.

Ready to get started?

15 Ideas for Using LinkedIn

1 Start by following the general social media guidelines mentioned earlier, including using your real name (not just the last initial for your last name), a proper headshot, and so on. Read or watch some instructional videos before you begin.

2 Turn off notifications to your network immediately, or your network will see every edit and change you make to your profile. Also turn off email notifications if you don't want to receive a lot of emails.

3 Load your resume onto LinkedIn if you want a quick way to populate your profile. LinkedIn will translate your resume into its profile structure. This is a great way to get started, but don't limit yourself to just what LinkedIn creates. You will need to fix it up.

4 Write a strong headline. What are the key things you want to be known for? Keep keywords in mind. Read other people's profiles to get ideas.

5 The summary section is an opportunity for another conversation with a potential employer. What do you want to tell the employer about yourself?

6 To enhance your profile and show off your skills, you can upload rich media: hyperlinks, documents, papers, articles, writing samples, presentations you completed for classes or internships, and portfolios.

7 Use the skills and endorsements section by putting in about ten key skills you hope others will endorse you for. Don't waste too much time in this area, however. Many employers don't trust the public endorsements.

8 Join groups related to your desired profession (you can join up to one hundred). Monitor your group communication settings, however, so you're not sending and/or receiving too many emails. Post intelligent questions and join groups where you will stand out. Start conversations by sharing interesting articles related to your field of study or your career field. Notice who responds to your postings and connect with them.

9 Follow companies that interest you. Look up the profile page of any company you're interested in. Notice if anyone from your network works there. Check to see if any alumni from your school work there. Read the profiles of the individuals who have jobs you're interested in.

You will get a good idea of the experience and education that employer is seeking for those titles.

10 Follow thought-leaders and influencers in your field of interest.

11 Click JobsLink on the top navigation bar to set up email alerts for jobs related to your interests (Linkedin.com/directory/jobs).

12 Use keywords to find the jobs most related to your interests. You can search jobs by title, name of company, geographic location, or even a job function. For instance, if you want a job where you have a chance to use your knowledge of Italian, simply put "Italian" as one of your keywords.

13 Avoid following political figures unless you are seeking a career related to politics. Always keep your desired audience in mind: employers. Don't link to or follow anyone who might conflict with your desired employment. Controversy generally doesn't play well in the job search.

14 Add connections. Look for people who might be interested in connecting with you. Start with alumni from your school who are in the career field you seek or who majored in the same subject as you. Use the alumni tool to find alumni from your school by using https://www.linkedin.com/alumni, which will take you to your most recent school from your profile. You can then search how many alumni from your school are on LinkedIn, where they live and where they work, and so on.

15 Always write a personal note when connecting. Don't just hit the Connect button. Write to the person and let them know why you're connecting. For example, "I enjoyed reading your post on trends in art gallery management and I'd like to connect with you."

Once you've completed your basic profile, before you make it public, use the following rubric to make sure you haven't missed something.

LinkedIn Rubric For Job Seekers

	COMPETITIVE	SATISFACTORY	NEEDS IMPROVEMENT
Picture	• Professional headshot • Clear and non-distracting background • Attire appropriate for field	• Professional appearance, but background poor • Unprofessional attire	• No picture or unprofessional • Picture with someone cut out
Headline	• Focuses on titles, skills, and keywords for industry • Articulates specific goal • Indicates what seeking	• Some title and skills listed • Indicates college major only • No mention of industry or professional goal	• "Student at . . ." • Just indicates "seeking job" • Doesn't highlight skills or expertise
"About" Section (Summary)	• Clear description of skills, strengths, and accomplishments • Uses relevant keywords to target industry • Follows and enhances resume	• Describes skills and achievements, but too short (lacks detail) or too long	• No summary • Poorly written or contains misspellings • Discrepancy between resume and content
Experience	• Relevant skills, responsibilities, or achievements highlighted • No typos or grammar issues • Dates accurate and current • Uses keywords and language relevant to target industry • Lists volunteer, student organizations, etc.	• Lists main skills and responsibilities, is either incomplete or too detailed	• Leaves out key information • No description of skills, responsibilities, or achievements • Dates are missing or confusing • Typos or grammatical errors

continued →

	COMPETITIVE	SATISFACTORY	NEEDS IMPROVEMENT
Education	• Includes institution, degree, major, and years of attendance • Includes other relevant training programs, including high school (for networking purposes) • Other relevant information included	• Lists high school and college but provides no details	• Failure to list colleges or other education • Dates are missing or confusing
Skills and Recommendations	• Skills are relevant to target industry • Skills are described in experience or other sections • Skills are endorsed by others • Recommendations are visible	• Skills listed, but not all relevant to target industries • Recommendations are provided, but not relevant for target industries	• No skills listed in the skill section • No recommendations

Cover Letters

Just like your social media profile, a cover letter is an attempt to start a conversation in writing with a potential employer. The cover letter provides a chance for you to explain to an employer why you would be a great employee. You get to tell your story in a deeper way than through your resume. You are starting to develop a relationship with the employer through the letter.

Create your cover letter with three to four paragraphs. It should not be longer than one page. You have three points to make: introducing yourself and the opportunity/organization you're seeking (first paragraph); expanding important information about yourself (beyond the resume) that would interest the employer and connects directly to the position (second and possibly third paragraph); and identifying the next action step (final paragraph).

The old concept of a cover letter is a paper document you send in the mail with your resume. That's pretty much gone now, but it is still common to write a cover letter and simply send it as a PDF or Word document along with your resume. If that's what you're doing, you will want to follow traditional cover letter advice. But in addition to the traditional cover letter, there is a hybrid that some call an "e-note" or "email cover," with the idea that it's the email you send along with your resume. In this case, your e-note will be shorter than a traditional cover letter, but you will still want it to cover the basics.

Just keep in mind that the word on cover letters is mixed. Some employers say they don't read them. Others say they rely more on what's in the cover letter than the resume, and view the cover letter as a great way to evaluate the candidate's writing skills (an important competency, if you recall). Others say they are a waste of time.

So what are you supposed to do?

Write the best cover letter you can for the situation. Yes, it might be ignored. But it might be the ticket that gets you into the interview. So take it seriously and take your time in writing it. If you write one, make it the best example of your writing that you can. The point of the letter is to connect the dots between you and this future job. Everything in your letter should support that.

Writing the cover letter is also a great exercise in career confirmation; if you're having trouble explaining why you're right for the job, maybe you aren't. Are you having to stretch too much to find a connection? Maybe you're even stretching the truth about your skills or interests. (For instance, maybe the position requires close attention to details and strong organizational skills, and you really don't like details and your room is pretty messy. Are you sure you really want this job?) As you write your letter, take note of your energy level. Are you getting excited about connecting yourself to this position? Or are you getting tired or losing interest? Your energy level may be a valuable clue to your true interest in the position.

Here are ten guidelines for writing a cover letter that will help sell you in the job search:

1   You don't have to do this alone. Your career center can help you with your cover letter at every stage. Many centers have drop-in hours where you can bring your letter for a review.

2   Read the job description of the position you're seeking. Jot down the keywords and competencies and plan to use them in your letter.

3   Before you write, take a few moments to think about your skills, interests, and values—all the information you gathered into your Backpack. Then, think about this position you're seeking. How do you fit? How do your skills or experiences align with what the employer is seeking? If there's not a perfect one-to-one match, how can you explain the similarities? And don't worry if you can't connect everything. Few candidates can. Just connect the important aspects of the job with your experience and education.

4   Focus on what the employer wants (which hopefully matches what you have to offer). Connect the dots so the employer can see you have the ability to do the job. Think about your skills in terms of what a situation was, how you handled it, and what the outcome was.

5   Stay positive in your tone and be careful not to lead with your weaknesses. Instead of writing, "Although I don't have your desired years of experience . . . ," write "My experiences over the past three years align well with what you are seeking. . . ." Focus on what you do have, not what you don't.

6   Use the name and title of intended recipient. Avoid "To Whom It May Concern" or "Dear Sir or Madam." If you must use an anonymous greeting, consider something like "Dear Hiring Manager" or "Greetings." Search the company website or LinkedIn to find the name of HR staff person or the hiring manager for the position.

7   Customize each letter. You can have a general template to work from, but do more than just change the name of the company or the job title. Employers can spot form letters easily. Take the time to personalize your letter. Let them know you've done your research.

8   Use your cover letter to bring up experiences or skills that might not be in your resume. Use your sentences to explain and verify your competencies. ("I have strong teamwork experience through my work on a project. . . .")

9   Review your sentences for structure, grammar, and readability. Make sure you have no spelling errors. Do not start every sentence with "I."

10 End your letter with a clear statement of what should happen next. Make sure your cell phone and email are in the last paragraph of your letter, just in case it is separated from your resume.

COVER LETTER RUBRIC

Have you written a cover letter? Try comparing it with this rubric to see if it's ready to be sent to a potential employer.

	COMPETITIVE	SATISFACTORY	NEEDS IMPROVEMENT
Format and salutation	• Follows standard business letter format, including a date, salutation, and signature • Personalized name and address of recipient • Organized and well-written • Good grammar • Varied sentence structure • Conveys interest and enthusiasm • One page long	• Follows most standard business letter practices • Fails to identify the name or title of recipient • Overuse of "I" to start sentences • One page long	• Fails to follow standard business letter format • Not well organized • Poor grammar and misspellings • Difficult to read or understand • Confusing sentences • Doesn't express interest or enthusiasm • Two pages long
First Paragraph	• States purpose • Identifies the position sought • Opens with an interesting sentence • Explains any connection to the company • Cites how candidate learned of job • Quickly identifies common connections between candidate and position	• Opens with "I am a senior majoring in . . ." • Mentions position but doesn't explain where learned of position • Omits a connection between the candidate and the position • Mentions a strength not related to position	• Doesn't state the position sought • Focuses just on the candidate's interests, not the organization's • Fails to convey interest or enthusiasm about position • Enters wrong company or position

continued →

Cover Letter Rubric (continued)

	COMPETITIVE	SATISFACTORY	NEEDS IMPROVEMENT
Middle Paragraph(s)	• Provides information about candidate skills, knowledge, experience, and interests specifically in relation to the position sought • Uses keywords related to position • Connects self to organization and position	• Provides less relevant information • Doesn't focus on skills and knowledge that relate to the position • Provides unnecessary information	• Repeats information in resume • Doesn't back up skill statements with examples • Provides little insight or new info for employer • Fails to engage reader • Fails to demonstrate knowledge of company or position
Final Paragraph	• Thanks the reader for reading • Expresses interest in continuing the conversation • Provides contact information for candidate • Offers to contact company or expresses desire for company to contact candidate (adjusted for field)	• Thanks the reader for reviewing • Doesn't provide follow-up plans related to field	• Doesn't thank reader or provide contact information • Doesn't indicate what possible next steps might be taken

CHAPTER 8

Establish Significant Conversations

Pitches, Networking, and Interviewing

———

Three conversations and a pitch can land you a job.

What does that mean? What conversations? Well, Richard Bolles realized that certain words, like "network" and "interview," conjure up all sorts of resistance and bad feelings. Almost no one likes to be told to "network." Isn't that an awkward, forced interaction that everyone tells you you're supposed to do?

And interviewing? Well, you would not be alone if the thought of an interview makes you tense up, maybe start sweating a little, and begin worrying if you'll ever get a job.

But a conversation? A conversation is just two people talking. It's just sharing information back and forth. It's about finding an easy way to build a connection or establish a relationship that might end up benefitting you. You have conversations every day. No big deal. That's how I want you to think about the various interviews and networking opportunities you will encounter in your job search. What starts with two people talking can quickly turn into a powerful network that can connect you to more career opportunities than you can imagine.

And the pitch? That's just a short speech you create for when you're asked "tell me about yourself." Also called an "elevator pitch" (because it should be short enough that you can complete it during a ride on an elevator), it's a way for you to quickly identify to a potential employer your key skills and strengths and the work you desire.

Here's a secret you might not know: if you're a college student, you are in the best position possible to develop your network. You have access to lots of alumni who want to give back to their school, and you can take advantage of student rates in professional organizations that give you access to local meetings, job listings, and conferences (more on that later). People want to help college students. They understand that you are eager to learn and have lots of ideas about your future. They enjoy sharing their experiences with you and providing the guidance they might not have received. Can you see that you already have an advantage over other job seekers just by virtue of being enrolled in college? Not only that, you have access to all sorts of social media where unique connections can happen in a second once you know how to take advantage of it.

So let's break this process down to make it easier and less stressful. We'll examine the kinds of conversations and pitches that will help you in the job-search process. To keep it simple, we're going to look at four levels of conversations, based on the amount of time they take, the level of preparation required, and the seriousness of their purpose. Level 1 is a basic conversation, Level 2 is your pitch, Level 3 is an information-focused conversation (information interview), and Level 4 is a job-related conversation (job interview).

Level 1: The Art of Basic Conversation

Throughout the day you probably have lots of conversations. Maybe with your professor to clarify a due date for a paper. Or with someone you happen to sit next to at a concert where you share your mutual love for the performer. Or the person on the treadmill next to you who has also signed up for an upcoming 5K. Or the person you meet at a protest for a cause you believe in. Or your job at the local coffee shop requires you to take customer orders. These are friendly conversations, often with strangers, with whom you have a moment of connection or mutual interest. Most of the time they pass by unnoticed. But every once in a while, they become more. That's because you never know who has the power to help you with your plans. Engaging in these simple conversations could be the ticket to your future.

For some people, conversations come easily. Maybe you're just naturally a "people person." I once worked with a recruiter whose job was to find new employers for our students. A natural connector, she made a new employer connection standing on a street corner at a particularly long red light. While waiting for the walk-light, she noticed the person next to her was dressed in a nice suit. She complimented him and asked him what type of work he did. Turned out, he worked for a company she had been hoping to bring to campus for student interviews. She quickly introduced herself and started talking about the school she represented (it turned out his brother was a graduate). By the time they had crossed the street, they had exchanged business cards and she had snared a new employer for her students.

Now maybe that's you—you have all sorts of interesting encounters with people. And if that's the case, skip this section and move on to working on your pitch.

But maybe that's not you. Maybe the fine art of conversation doesn't sound appealing at all. You'd much rather hide inside your earbuds and stare at your phone. And that's okay. It just won't help you connect and land your parachute. So let's work on this. Start by rating your anxiety or stress level about initiating conversations:

1	2	3	4	5
Highly anxious. I really hate the thought of doing these exercises. I feel anxious when I have to initiate conversations.	**Somewhat anxious.** I'm introverted or shy and find it uncomfortable to reach out to strangers.	**I'm neutral about conversations.** My anxiety depends on the situation.	**Mostly comfortable.** I generally enjoy talking to people, even when I don't know them.	**Very comfortable.** I'm a social butterfly. I love to meet new people and easily reach out to them.

Take note of your rating. If your stress level is comfortable (#4 or #5), then you probably enjoy these conversations—maybe you even seek them out and start them yourself. So just keep doing what you're doing.

But if gave yourself a 3 or less, take a minute to analyze yourself. Is it because you don't like talking to strangers? Or are all interactions difficult? The harder this type of interaction is, the more you will need to practice it. (I know that's not what you wanted to hear.) But by practicing, you will get better at it, and you will greatly increase your chance of success in the job search. If you can't get comfortable interacting with people, you will be held back in your ability to get a job. Practice will improve your conversational skills. You might even discover it isn't as awful as you think. (A great resource to check out is the book *Quiet: The Power of Introverts in a World That Can't Stop Talking* by Susan Cain. An introvert who successfully mastered the extroverted MBA program at Harvard, Cain offers lots of insights on how to manage yourself in a world full of extroverts.)

Getting used to small, unimportant conversations is important because they will help you handle the more important conversations later. Small conversations are an important aspect of communication, and while they seem so simple, they can actually be hard to do with everyone on their cell phones and earbuds. The art of making small talk is dying, and if you have it, you will stand out in social situations, like job interviews and networking receptions.

Here are some tips for starting and practicing these casual interactions. Next time you're standing in line, in an elevator, sitting at a concert, or otherwise stuck next to a person.

- **Compliment them.** Look for something neutral you like. Perhaps it's the color of a scarf or a piece of jewelry the person is wearing. Or a cool tattoo. That's it. Just compliment, the person will say thank you, and you're done.

- **Notice a book or other item the stranger is holding.** Does the person like that book? What's it about? Does the person recommend it? If you want, recommend a similar book you like. Again, that's the end. All you're doing is practicing basic conversational skills.

- **Ask about the person's favorite sports team,** if you notice a team shirt or cap. Is this person a fan? Does the person have a favorite player? Mention what team you like. (Keep it light—this isn't about rivalries.)

- **Comment on the place you're in.** "I can't believe the long line today. It's usually not this bad." Or "Have you tried their new coffee flavor (or whatever is new on the menu)?" Once again, you'll likely get a one-word response. That's fine. This practice is about you, not them.

- **Comment on the weather.** Hot, cold, too much rain, too little rain, and so on. Just saying, "Isn't it a beautiful day?" or "What crazy weather today!" is enough.

Here's a goal: every day this week start up a conversation with a stranger. (Make sure you're in a public area and don't talk to anyone you get a troublesome vibe from. Keep it light and friendly, but not overly interested. This is not a book about dating.)

Remember these little conversations are just designed to make you more comfortable with small talk. Nothing will come of them other than you will gradually reduce your anxiety about approaching strangers, have a short pleasant interaction, and develop the amazingly powerful skill of small talk.

• • •

Tamara was stuck in an endless line at the campus coffee shop. She kept checking her phone, worried she'd be late for the next class. Looking around at the line, she suddenly noticed the woman behind her was carrying a satchel she liked. It was stuffed with papers and books. She gritted her teeth, knowing she was "supposed" to practice this small talk stuff. So she took a breath and said, "I love your satchel—I have one like it at home and it's my favorite." The woman smiled broadly and started talking about how she found it at an outlet store just outside of town. That started a conversation about outlet shopping. The line inched forward, and Tamara ordered her coffee. As she started to leave the line, the woman asked her if she was a student. Tamara said, "Yes, I'm an English major. I really want to get into the creative writing program but it's super-competitive." The woman looked at her. "I teach in that program. Stop by my office this afternoon and bring some samples of your writing. Let's talk."

• • •

Courage.
Eye contact.
Sincerity.
A compliment.
Pleasantness.
Who knows what might happen?

Level 2: Making a 30-Second Pitch

The 30-second (or elevator) pitch is something you will want to prepare and practice. Having a strong pitch can serve as a great introduction to a potential employer, a way to respond to the "tell me about yourself" kind of question, or even just a way to introduce yourself at a career fair or networking event. Your pitch needs to grab the listener's attention and be short enough and interesting enough to make the listener want to hear more.

Here is the traditional elevator pitch most students create:

"I'm a senior at _____ University majoring in _____. I'm seeking a career in _____."

It's okay, but not too enticing, unless the person you're speaking with is specifically interested in your school, your major, or your career plans.

But there's a different frame for your pitch:

- Think about time span.
- Identify what you can say about yourself in the present, past, and future.
- Incorporate keywords from your field (see chapters 5 and 6 for more information) into your pitch.

I'm currently studying _____, which I became interested in _____, and I hope to continue my research by working in _____ in the future.

Here's another frame to try. Focus on what you do and what you hope to do at the event you're currently attending:

I'm an intern at _____ and I'm really enjoying my work with _____, so I'm hoping to meet people here who can help me learn more about careers in _____.

Those are more like 10-second pitches, which might be just right for the situation. But you could take the frame and expand a little more, as in the next example.

• • •

Sophie is attending a local meeting of *The Society of Human Resource Management*. She's a student member of the organization and decided to attend the meeting to meet people in the field. Here's her pitch:

"Hi, my name is Sophie Jones. I'm currently studying English at Ohio State University and I plan to become a lawyer. But first I'd really like to work in a human resources office to get a better understanding of labor law. I'm particularly interested in regulatory compliance and union-management negotiation. That's what I plan to specialize in. I'm curious, is that something you might have some thoughts about?"

● ● ●

In this pitch, Sophie has (1) identified herself and her current situation, (2) indicated her future plans, (3) provided a specific area of interest including keywords, and (4) asked for help. This pitch has great potential for the setting she's in. She will likely modify it for other settings, like a career fair. Notice she's not asking for a job; she's asking for an opinion or information. She will likely get a lot of helpful information and maybe even a connection to a possible internship or job.

Now it's time to develop your pitch. Which of the models on the facing page do you like best? Think of it this way:

What do you want to say about your current situation?

_____

What have you done in the past that is relevant and adds to your pitch?

_____

What are the relevant keywords to include?

_____

What do you want to say about your future?

_____

What do you want the listener to help you with?

_____

Play around with your pitch. Jot down several ideas and try saying them out loud. Which pitch sounds the best and fits your needs?

Write your final pitch here, in your notebook, or on your computer. (Don't assume you will remember it. You won't.)

_____

_____

_____

A Brief Pause before We Move to the 3rd and 4th Level of Conversations

Congratulations! You've mastered the art of small talk, and you've developed your pitch. Now you're ready to tackle more challenging information-focused conversations and job-related conversations. But—don't confuse the two. It's a major mistake that can scuttle your networking efforts.

Information interviews are for information. Job interviews are for jobs. Yes, there are times that one turns into the other, but for now, keep the boundaries straight.

Let's say you get a phone call from a student who goes to your high school. The student would like to attend your college and asks if you can tell him about your experience. Of course you will. You'll tell him everything you can think of. What you like about it. What majors are the best. What the parties are like. Why you would or wouldn't choose it again. And so on. All is wonderful. That's an information conversation (information interview).

Then the student suddenly says, "Can you get me into your college?" Hmm. That's a conversation-stopper isn't it? Chances are, you don't have the power to get someone into your school. You might be able to tell the admissions office about the student, but that's about it. Right? Now you're not feeling so good about this conversation. Maybe you feel a little bad that you can't help more. Now it's awkward, and you'll probably end the call.

Can you see the difference between seeking information and making a specific request that's out of your purview? Maybe you're a tour guide on your campus, and you have a special "in" with the admissions office. So you might, on your own, offer to help the student by putting in a good word for him. And you and the student will feel great, but that's the difference: you offered rather than been asked. Keep this analogy in mind when you read about the next two levels of conversations, that is, interviews.

Level 3: Information-Focused Conversations—Information Interviewing and Networking

You've no doubt heard about the value of developing a network. During the job search process you will have the opportunity to have a lot of conversations with people who can help you. You never know what can come of this type of conversation. And quite often these conversations are unplanned and unexpected.

• • •

Daniel, a junior economics major, was struggling with his career plans. Most of his friends were looking at finance and data analytics careers. Making a lot of money seemed to be their primary goal, but Daniel didn't think the same way. Despite good grades that would give him an entry to those fields, he just wasn't interested. He had struggled with ADHD throughout school, and the thought of having to focus on numbers and statistics all day sounded worse than school. It was hard enough to sit still in a one-hour class much less on an eight-hour-a-day job. While visiting campus on family weekend, his mother volunteered to attend a "career conversations" event where she would talk to students about her career. Daniel, hoping to get a nice lunch afterward, tagged along. He got bored and wandered around the room, where he discovered a table labeled "Health Care Careers." Three parents were sitting there alone. He said hello and, just to be pleasant, asked them what they did. One was a nurse, the other a doctor, but the third person said, "I work for a behavioral management institute. We help children and adults improve their focus and attention so they can do better in school and work." Daniel was intrigued. He'd never heard of this type of center. He sat down and they started talking and having an information-focused conversation. He learned one of their missions was to reduce the need for medications by changing the behavior of each client. Daniel felt a personal attachment to that; he had struggled his whole life with medications for his ADHD. By the end, he had a business card, an appointment for a follow-up phone call, and an invitation to do an internship in the summer. Daniel didn't know for sure, but he thought he just might be on his way to an interesting career.

• • •

This example not only illustrates the power of networking and information interviewing but demonstrates how simple it can be. Richard

Bolles deserves credit for greatly enhancing the concept of the "information interview," conversations designed to help you connect to potential employers. In these conversations you are seeking information from the other person. You could be seeking their knowledge about a career field or job, or about the place where they live, or any other information that might be helpful to you in your search. There are lots of opportunities to have these types of conversations, and they're not as hard to set up as you might think.

Here's how to get started when you have a lead on an alumnus or another person you have identified as a possible source for help:

1 Identify the purpose of your conversation. Use this Thought Organizer to outline possible questions for an information interview about a career field you're considering:

WHAT DO YOU ALREADY KNOW ABOUT THIS CAREER FIELD OR COMPANY?	WHAT DON'T YOU KNOW (AND NEED TO KNOW) ABOUT THIS FIELD OR ORGANIZATION?	WHY IS THIS INFORMATION IMPORTANT? HOW WILL YOU USE IT? WHAT DECISIONS MIGHT IT INFORM?

2 Reach out with an email first. Be sure to personalize it to the person and their organization or the connection you have with them. Decide whether you are requesting to meet them in-person, on the phone, or virtually.

3 Prepare several questions in advance. This is a great opportunity to get the inside scoop on an industry, organization, or position. Get the interviewee's opinions beyond what you can learn on the internet. (You can say something such as, "I was reading the website and it says your company offers _____. Can you tell me more about that?" or "I was reading that a keyword in your industry is _____. Can you help me understand that?") You can also ask the person about their educational background and what their job is like. Two

great questions to ask toward the end are "Do you have any advice for me about entering this career field?" and "Is there anyone else I should speak to about this?"

4 If you're meeting them, it's okay to take a friend with you if you're nervous about the process. If you have a friend who has the same career interests, bring your friend along.

5 Keep the conversation short. After ten to fifteen minutes, thank the interviewee and say you don't want to take more time. If the person wants to keep talking, though, let it happen.

6 End by asking whether there is someone else you should speak with, give your thanks for the time spent with you, and then follow up with a thank-you email or note.

Now that you know how an information interview might benefit you, how do you go about finding someone to interview? Here are ten resources to tap for career information and networking conversations.

1 **University-related.** Professors, fellow students, and event speakers are potentially great resources you can start tapping immediately. Alumni are another relatively easy connection. Look to connect with alumni with whom you have something in common such as major, athletic team, Greek organization, club, musical or theatre groups, and so on. Look for alumni who live in a geographic area where you'd like to live, or are in the career field you're considering.

2 **Parents.** Your future career might be helped by the parents of your roommate or your friends. You never know. Start with your residence hall. Find out what occupations exist among the parents of the students on your floor. Make a point of meeting the parents when they come to a campus weekend. Or, ask your roommate or friends if you could speak with their parents about their careers.

3 **High school connections.** Consider returning for your high school homecoming weekend. Go to the football game or whatever other events might be going on. Wear a shirt with your college logo—it's a great conversation-starter. Tell everyone you meet what you're majoring in and/or the career you're considering. Remember, you have changed since high school and your friends have, too. They might have a connection now that could be helpful. And, always give back. If one of your friends shares a career interest and you know someone at your school who could help them, share that connection.

4 Geographic connections. Sometimes you know people because of a specific place you once lived or visited frequently. Maybe you spent your summers at a relative's house in the city or in the country or on a beach. Because of that, you met new people you wouldn't normally interact with. Well, now those people are part of your network so take advantage of that. Investigate what career fields they are in (if you don't already know). Contact them, remind them of how they know you, and see if you can arrange a phone conversation about their career and suggestions they might have for you.

5 LinkedIn or other social media connections. As you learned in chapter 7, social media is an amazingly efficient and potentially invaluable source of new connections. Social media levels the playing field for anyone who doesn't have a built-in network. Let's say you want to work for an advocacy group. You're particularly interested in environmental issues. But no one you know is in this field. Well, social media can get you connected quickly. Start by following key environmental groups on Twitter, Facebook, Instagram, and any other similar platforms. Select local as well as national or international organizations. Read what they post, looking for potential opportunities to connect. "Like" and share their posts with your followers. If you see a local volunteer event, show up. Find out who the organizers are and introduce yourself. Do a great job volunteering, and they'll likely ask you to volunteer again. From there, you can transition to an internship and maybe ultimately a job. (If you haven't read it yet, go to chapter 7 for more information on social media.)

6 Professional organizations. Bet you didn't think about this one. Virtually every profession has at least one professional organization related to their field. Whether it's the American Marketing Association or the Association of Zoos and Aquariums, you will find a tremendous source of potential job information by joining as a student member. Even if you can't or don't join, their websites often contain lots of free information about careers, lists of members (which can be a great resource for finding potential employers), job postings, and so on. Many publish online newsletters that can be a source of information about trends, key people, or the latest news in the field. Just Google your desired career field and "professional organizations." See what shows up.

7 Former supervisors and colleagues. You are connected to them from internships, summer jobs, and volunteer experiences. Again, you never know who they might know. So if they haven't seen you in a while or don't know your latest career plans, contact them. Tell them what you're doing now, and ask if they have any suggestions for you or know people you might be able to talk to.

8 **Local companies and organizations.** In whatever town or city your college is located, there are bound to be companies that work in your field of interest. They may be small or not directly related, but never underestimate the value of their connections. If you're interested in advertising, look around for local advertising agencies. Stop in and ask if you can meet with someone for ten minutes to talk about the organization. Sometimes just having a nice conversation with the front-desk person can be valuable. They may know other agencies you could speak with or may help you get an appointment with one of the staff.

9 **Company representatives.** Students don't always realize that a career fair isn't just for finding a job; it's also about gathering information. Even if you're a first-year student and not seeking a job, consider going to the career fair and wandering through the various employer booths. Note how it works, find an employer no one is speaking with, and walk up and say hi. Explain that you're just exploring careers and ask what they do. You might be surprised to learn the wide variety of opportunities at an organization.

10 **People you know through hobbies and activities.** Maybe you have sung in your church choir for many years. Do you know the occupations of the other people in the choir? Perhaps you have been going to same gym for a while. What about the people you see all the time? What type of work do they do? Here's your chance to try that small talk and see what develops.

Level 4: The Career or Job-Related Conversation (Also Known as a Job Interview)

Now we're ready for the biggest conversation of all—the job interview. And, yes, it is still a conversation, albeit with more layers of importance and stress added on. But you're a skilled conversationalist at this point, right? You've mastered the casual conversation and the information-focused conversation, and you're ready to ratchet up your skills.

One way to think about this conversation is to look at it from the potential employer's point of view. Try thinking like an interviewer throughout the process. What are the interviewer's concerns, what might "worry" the interviewer about you, and how can you mitigate that? What do you think the interviewer is seeking? What strengths do you have that the interviewer will be interested in or should know about?

Here's an interesting fact you should know before you go to an interview: employers don't always trust the skills of college students. A survey conducted by the American Association of Universities and Colleges, reported in *Inside Higher Ed*, found that students give themselves much higher scores on workplace competencies than employers do. Across all competencies surveyed, employers ranked the college students' abilities lower than the students did themselves.[7] The biggest discrepancies were in the areas of oral and written communication, critical thinking, and being creative where students were "twice as likely as employers to think that students are being well-prepared." Given employers' suspicions, it is imperative that you provide behavioral examples (and stories) that demonstrate your skills. (See chapter 10 if you need to build up your skills and experience through internships or other short-term experiences.)

One way to get inside the mind of an employer is to review a typical evaluation form an interviewer might complete following your interview.

Let's break down each of these components of the interview and make sure you're at your best throughout.

1   **Appearance.** Your first few seconds in an interview are extremely important. Before you say a word, your overall appearance will be evaluated. This means you need to be properly dressed for the interview. Here are some quick ideas to help you give the best first impression.

- Wear clothes that are appropriate for the employment setting you're seeking. Conservative suit for business/finance/consulting interviews. Business casual for nonprofit or educational organizations. Check your career center's website for any links related to interview clothing choices. Many career centers post recommended clothing guidelines for various events, including career fairs and on-campus recruiting.

- Everything you wear should be clean and neatly pressed. (No getting your slacks off the floor of your closet.)

- Women's clothing should be business professional in nature. No cocktail dresses, low necklines, super-short or tight skirts or slacks, overdone jewelry or makeup. Men should avoid suits that are too tight to move comfortably, throwing a blazer over a T-shirt, or shoes that are too casual.

- If you identify as LGBTQ+ and don't align yourself with traditional masculine or feminine wardrobe styles, check out the helpful tips and guidelines from Alison Doyle at The Balance Careers (https://www.thebalancecareers.com/gender-neutral-interview-and-business-clothing-2061166).

- Always check with your career center if you have any questions. Consider bringing (or wearing) your outfit to the center for suggestions.

- If you can't afford interview clothing, see if you can borrow from a friend who wears your size. Also, check with your career center. Some centers have clothing closets or offer discounts or gift cards for clothing stores. Local thrift shops and Goodwill centers often have great interview outfits at a low cost. Check online clothing sites for deep discounts; often an online retail store will sell remaining clothes from the previous season at up to 70 percent off the retail price. For women, the not-for-profit organization Dress for Success (https://dressforsuccess.org) provides clothing for interviews at affiliate programs across the country.

Your appearance doesn't just involve clothing. Nervous mannerisms can ruin the impression you make even if you answer every question well. Quite often the only way you will know that you have these issues is if you record yourself in a mock interview setting. You can do this on your cell phone—place the phone far enough away that you can see all of yourself, not just your face. Practice answering a few basic questions ("Tell me about yourself." "What are your best strengths?" "Tell me a time when you had to overcome a problem.") Then play back the recording. Cringe all you want (yes, most of us don't like watching ourselves like this), but watch carefully. You can listen to your answers, of course. But also turn off the volume and just watch yourself.

- Are you noticing any nervous mannerisms you want to stop? If you know you have a habit of moving your hands or twisting your hair or tapping your feet, find a way to reduce that. Fold your hands in your lap. Place both feet on the floor and don't move them much.

- If you are interviewing virtually, note the camera angle. Keep a direct focus on your face to limit the view of your hands.

- Are your facial expressions appropriate—not too flat and unexpressive and not too dramatic? (If you have a disability that affects your facial expressions or voice tone, you might want to mention this to the interviewer. You can introduce this casually by saying something like, "You might think I'm not excited based on my expressions, but that's just a function of my neurodiversity. I am genuinely excited about this opportunity and would greatly enjoy learning more about it." If this is an ongoing issue for you, check with your disability services office for assistance. An article titled "Navigating Social Skills in the Workplace" from Open Doors Therapy is helpful, and can be found at https://opendoorstherapy.com/navigating-social-skills-in-the-workplace-facial-expressions.

  Remember, you don't have to be a statue; just be aware of and reduce nervous movements as much as you can.

2 **Resume.** Check out chapter 6 for everything you need to know about your resume. Bring along extra copies to your interview just in case not everyone you meet has a copy.

3 **Interpersonal skills.** Interpersonal skills are hard to define, but they include being friendly, smiling, shaking hands, making small talk, and just generally demonstrating that you're an enjoyable person to be around. The good news is you've already practiced these skills through the conversation practice and information interviews. As a result, you're going to feel more relaxed and confident than your friends. Stay polite throughout the entire time of the interview and acknowledge everyone at the interview site (including the front-desk person). Practice shaking hands—try it out with your friends or roommate. Ask for feedback: too soft, too strong, and so on. A weak handshake can start the interview off on a bad note that might be hard to recover from.

    Balance listening with speaking. The number-one mistake made in interviews is talking too much or too little. That may seem hard to define exactly but aim for 50 percent talking and 50 percent listening. Remember, this is a conversation and you're trying to learn as much as you can about the position and the organization, just as they are trying to learn as much as they can about you. And it is ultimately a conversation. Conversations are all about give and take—not one side monopolizing the conversation.

4   **Knowledge of position, skills to perform job well, communication, and leadership potential.** Now here's the meat of the conversation. You can shine through this part if you do your homework and practice. This is not the place to wing it. You will need to be prepared with research and with practiced responses to typical questions. Remember, in addition to getting a job offer, your goal is to learn more about the position and the organization, determine if it still fits, and if you want to be hired. While not all interviews and interviewers are the same, you can expect to get typical questions; particularly in your first interview with an organization.

General Questions and Questions Based on Your Resume

- **Tell me about yourself.** This is the most common question. Be prepared with a short synopsis of your work or school experience.

- **Tell me about your most recent job.** Always speak positively about any work experience. Focus on the skills you acquired and what you learned. Prepare a story that features a skill or challenge.

- **What did you major in and why?** Here's your chance to say something interesting about your major, particularly if it's not a typical major for the position. Be ready to articulate its value.

- **What was your favorite course and why?** Here's a chance to say something unique. You can focus on a course that's directly related to the position you're seeking, or if you have a good story, you can focus on a course that was interesting and state how what you learned applies to your current life.

- **Why are you interested in this position?** You must be knowledgeable about the position so you can frame the best response. Review the job posting prior to the interview and identify two or three key elements that match your experience, interests, or education.

- **What are you plans for the future?** Building knowledge, skills, and expertise. Focus on what opportunities might be at this organization. Don't mention future law or grad school unless it's relevant to the position.

More Specific Questions Tailored to the Job You're Seeking

- Tell me about your skills related to:

  - People
  - Technology
  - Managing projects
  - Handling problems
  - Working on a team
  - Working independently
  - Leadership
  - Data/Statistics
  - Math, accounting, or budgets

- Tell me about your knowledge of:

  - This position
  - Our organization
  - This field in general
  - Latest news or events in this field

Tips to Ace Those Important Conversations (Job Interviews)

Now that you know what the typical questions are (and don't be surprised when you hear atypical questions), you can start to prepare for your interview. There are three basic components to acing the content part of your interview: do your homework, know yourself and your strengths, and prepare stories for questions. Let's go in for a deeper dive.

DO YOUR HOMEWORK: RESEARCH

Have you ever been in class where someone asks a question they could have answered on their own if they had just read the assignment? Or asks something that could easily have been looked up on Google? How do you feel about those students? Yeah, that's what employers think, too. In fact, the number-one complaint of employers at career fairs is "They didn't do their research before talking with me." Don't be that person. Do your research.

Managing Phone Interviews

Phone interviews are increasingly common, particularly as screening interviews from a human resources (HR) office. When HR calls, they usually ask questions designed to verify that you have the basic qualifications needed to do the job. For instance, if the job requires that you use InDesign, they will likely ask about your use of InDesign. Then, if you pass the screening call, you might get another call from the person who would supervise you, or from another human resources representative.

Most of the time the employer will reach out to schedule a time, but sometimes you can get called at an unexpected time. If that's the case, you'll need to do some quick thinking. Are you able to handle the phone interview on the fly, or would it be better to reschedule? Consider your options.

- If you know it's the employer calling, and you're not ready, you can let it go to voice mail, listen to the message, and then call back when you're ready. (Don't allow much time to lapse however.)

- You can take the call and indicate that you would welcome the conversation but you're not at a place where you can do it right now. See if you can reschedule it.

- You can take the call, pull your resume up on your phone or your computer (whatever is available) so you have it as a reminder, and just do the interview.

- Knowing that you might get a phone call, you can keep a copy of each job description you've applied for in an easy-to-reach location. This could be a paper folder with a printout of the jobs, or a folder on your computer. Just having that information available can make your responses more to the point.

- Try to take the call in a relatively quiet location. Sit up or stand while talking so that you aren't too relaxed.

- Keep your responses succinct since you can't see the interviewer and can't read any non-verbal behaviors.

- Always be prepared to ask a few relevant questions about the position or the organization.

- At the end of the call, ask what the next step is in the process so you know what to expect from the employer.

- Read current articles, blog posts, or newspaper items about the organization and your field of interest.

- Check out the organization's website.

- Research information about your field of employment. What are the trends in the industry? Who are the key players?

- Read the job description thoroughly before the interview and identify key places where your skills and knowledge fit the position description.

Based on your research, you'll be able to ask intelligent questions when the employer asks what questions you have. Here are some questions to ask.

- Who succeeds in this position? What are the skills or traits of someone who is successful in this position or in this company? (And then match yourself to the response.)

- Ask about a specific division of the company you might want to work in later on in your career. For instance, maybe you're interested in the international division of a company even though you're currently applying for an entry-level position that won't involve that area.

- Ask the interviewer what they most enjoy about the organization.

Practice, Practice, Practice

It's easy to look at the above questions and think, "I can handle this." But it's a whole different story when you're at the interview, and you're alone in that room with your potential employer. The stakes are much higher, and preparation and practice are key. Do several mock interviews before the real one.

- Check with your career center and see if they offer mock interviews, either with their staff or through employers who provide them as a service.

- Check if online mock interviews are available. Career centers often purchase mock interview software or offer it as part of their job database services, like Handshake or Symplicity. While it won't be the same as an in-person mock interview, it's better than nothing.

- Give a list of potential interview questions to a friend, roommate, or classmate and ask for an interview. If you want to make it a little stressful, record the interview, so you can play it back and review it. The recording will help you treat the situation more seriously.

KNOW YOURSELF AND YOUR STRENGTHS

The good news here is you have already completed the Parachute exercises in chapters 2 and 3 that helped you identify your key strengths, skills, interests, and knowledge. You have identified the types of positions you want and the geographic areas where you want to live, and presumably the interviews you're preparing for are a good fit for you.

If you're not pursuing opportunities that interest you, stop a moment and ask yourself why you're interviewing. Your answer might be perfectly reasonable. If you're interviewing because you're interested in learning more or exploring a possible career, that's great. But if you're just interviewing because everyone else is, you're probably wasting your time. Go back and review everything you learned about yourself in chapters 1 to 4 and start researching opportunities that are a better fit for you.

Review the job description for key desired traits, skills, and knowledge. Match yourself to the position—be prepared to connect the dots from your background to the job.

What if you aren't a perfect match? Well, first of all, most people aren't. Assess which key skills you do have and focus on those. Indicate a desire to learn the others. Employers want smart people who can learn, so if you don't know something, just indicate a desire to learn.

Keep in mind that if there is virtually no connection between your skills/traits/knowledge and what the position is seeking, it's probably not worth your time to apply. Also, if the position is high up in an organization, and you're just getting out of college, again, it's likely not a great fit for you. Look to see if the same organization has more entry-level positions. Keep in mind that leadership skills in student organizations are excellent and valuable experiences, but they are not the same as working at a paid position. So while an employer will be interested in what you've done, a higher-level position is likely going to require someone with directly relevant paid work experience.

Be prepared for questions based on the content of your resume, cover letter, and LinkedIn page. Be ready to provide a good explanation of anything that you have provided. Pretend you're in a court of law and must justify why this job or this organization is right for you.

If you don't have a good story (or there isn't a good story) about a situation, try to leave it off your resume. What are your key argument points?

- Identify three to five key strengths you want to highlight at some point during the interview.
- Know why you are seeking the position you are interviewing for.

Five Tips for Managing a Virtual Interview

——

1 Research the company and position just like you would for a regular interview. Have your resume on a desk in front of you, preferably out of camera range.

2 Double-check the technology in advance. Turn off any distracting notifications or sounds that might interrupt. If possible, practice with the technology you'll be using. Log in a little early to the session to make sure your volume (microphone) and video (camera) settings are correct. Double-check the camera angle so that you are in focus. Have a back-up plan if the technology fails. If needed, be prepared to switch to audio-only. Have a phone number you can call if you get disconnected.

3 Check out your surroundings. Find a quiet space where you won't be disturbed. (Your career center or library might have quiet areas where you can conduct the interview.) Stay away from windows that might put a glare on you or your screen. Look for a neutral wall or other boring background. Turn off any equipment you're not using and close the door to the room. Place a "Do Not Disturb" sign on your door if you're in your dorm room.

4 Wear appropriate interview clothes from top to bottom even if the employer can only see your face. Our clothes affect our speaking style. If you're doing the interview in sweats and a T-shirt you're more likely to speak too casually or get too comfortable. You want to be a little uncomfortable—mild anxiety can improve your performance. Remember, the camera sees all. Make sure your clothing doesn't have strong patterns or bright colors that might strobe or glare. Wear solid dark colors, like navy blue, black, or dark gray.

5 Speak into the camera eye, particularly on a computer. If you look at the screen or keyboard, you won't be making eye contact with the interviewer. You don't have to stare them down, just remember to look at the camera when speaking.

- Have at least three stories prepared (see below) that illustrate your strengths.
- Use keywords related to the job in your stories.

PREPARE STORIES AND USE THE STAR TECHNIQUE

Stories provide evidence, proof that you can do what you say you can do. You can't predict the questions you'll be asked, but you can prepare stories and explanations that you can re-purpose to a variety of questions. Generally, the best storytellers get the best jobs. Many key industry leaders are great storytellers. They make their customers, workers, and investors want to support them.

But beware: stories don't just magically appear. You'll need to plan them in advance, and they require a lot of practice to tell smoothly. Don't tell a story for the first time in an interview. Try them out with your friends and get honest feedback. One way to get started is to review the stories you wrote in chapter 3. Are any of them potentially useful for an interview situation? Revise them as needed.

Your story must be relevant, not random. Know why you're telling a particular story. What skills, knowledge, or personal traits does this story emphasize? And why would an employer care about this? Consider success stories that focus on what you are proud of, where you were recognized for good work or talent, where you went beyond expectations and added value to a situation, where you created something new, or where you solved a problem. If you can add details that demonstrate outcomes, such as saving or making money, increasing number of clients or customers, or other related events, use them. Again, be sure to use keywords related to the position when creating your stories. For example, if the job description or advertisement mentions "team player" several times, you will want to tell a story about your success with a team.

One excellent method for telling a story is called the STAR technique. STAR stands for

- Situation
- Task
- Action
- Resolution

This is a great formula for thinking through a response to questions about how you solved problems, worked on teams, and created something. Here's one example in response to a question about your leadership skills.

Situation: *My school doesn't offer a marketing major, and I wanted to start a campus organization for students interesting in careers in marketing.*

Task: *In order to form the organization I had to determine how to best lead it.*

Action: *I created a list of ten tasks and worked through my list, starting with a conversation with my career center, which agreed to help me find business and alumni connections who could speak to the group. I also worked with the student affairs administrator who helped me form the organization and complete all the paperwork.*

Result: *Within two months, I officially formed the group, got it certified as an official student organization, created a leadership board (I'm the president), wrote a constitution and bylaws, and successfully recruited fifty students to the organization. We have already scheduled two speaker events, and we're working with the career center to bring more marketing-related employers to campus.*

Maybe your example will be a little less dramatic. For instance you might want to simply describe an incident at a summer job, or the time you helped a friend prepare for an exam. Using the STAR outline can help you shape an organized and focused story.

You can also use the STAR technique to answer the dreaded "weakness" question. Here's how Jose explained how he overcame a weakness at a summer job.

Situation: *I was at my summer job, and they asked me to use an Excel spreadsheet to organize a project, but I didn't know how to use it.*

Task: *I told them I didn't know, but that I would learn quickly. I asked if someone on the staff could assist me the next day.*

Action: *That evening at home, I watched several tutorials on YouTube and practiced setting up a basic spreadsheet.*

Result: *I brought in what I had worked on at home. Even though I wasn't an expert by any means on Excel, the staff member was impressed that I had shown such initiative and worked so hard on the project. He ended up writing me a great letter of recommendation at the end of the summer.*

It's Time To Create Your Stories

Take some time and jot down five potential interview stories. You can use the STAR framework if you'd like. Determine when you might use each story; what question that story might answer.

When you've written the outline of your stories, practice telling the story. Try using your phone to record the story and play it back. How long does it take? If it takes more than a minute to tell, you might want to work on making sure you've been as concise as possible. Do not tell a super-long (more than three-minute) story unless you have been asked to explain something in greater detail. A basic story that covers the important information is enough; the interviewer will ask for more information if needed.

Now that you've created your story, recorded it, and listened to it, does it meet the following parameters. My story is:

- Clear
- Concise
- Relevant to what is asked
- Keyword-based
- Significant in scope
- Positive
- Focused on my actions
- Interesting
- Enthusiastic

My story does not present me as:

- A know-it-all
- Arrogant
- Entitled
- A whiner, complainer, or blamer
- Negative

If it does, can I change the tone of the story, or should I find a different story?

Final Tips For Doing Well At Your Interviews

Before the interview:

- Practice always helps. For instance, if you're at a career fair, don't approach the companies you're most interested in first. You'll likely be too nervous. Select other companies where you can practice your skills and reduce your stress in what is a hectic environment. (And you never know—you might just like the company you were practicing on and decide to continue the conversation!)

- It can help to practice in the clothes you'll wear to the interview.

- Eat something before the interview but be sure to check your teeth. Carrying a small container of dental floss in your pocket or purse is always a good idea.

- Plan ahead—do you know where you're going? Arrive early even if you need to take a walk before you enter the site. Assume that from the moment you step foot in the parking lot, you might be observed. You never know who has a window above the parking lot and can watch what you do.

During the interview:

- Have a positive mindset. Remember, it's a conversation, not an interrogation.

- Watch your negative self-talk. You know that voice in your head that won't stop chattering. When you catch yourself getting stressed, try shrugging your shoulders or take deep, slow breaths. Sometimes just a few regulated breaths can go a long way to calm down your nervous system.

- Act as if you're confident even if you aren't. Remember you're an actor auditioning for a role. Channel your favorite superhero or movie star, the one who manages everything without a hitch.

- Focus on the interviewer, not on you. By keeping your attention on what the interviewer is saying and establishing this conversation, you won't be focusing as much on yourself.

- It's okay to pause after a question—you don't have to jump right in with an answer.

After the interview:

- Make it easy for the employer to contact you. Make sure your email and cell phone are on your resume and check them both regularly.

- Use the interview to improve future interviews. Jot down the questions you were asked (as best as you can remember; don't write them down during the interview). What did you answer well? What stories did you use? Did they work? Which questions were challenging? How would you change your answers next time?

- Identify two to three things you want to work on to improve at the next interview.

This chapter was fairly dense with a lot of important information. You might want to refer back to it throughout your search, particularly if you're finding job interviewing and networking challenging.

Remember, you don't have to do everything at once. Take it a step at a time by starting with a few friendly contacts to practice your new networking skills. Get feedback along the way and you'll soon develop the confidence to handle even difficult and challenging conversations.

A Special Case: Finance And Consulting Career Interviews

Not all interviews are the same; questions vary depending on the field. Those of you considering careers in finance and consulting need to be aware of the different types of interview questions you will be asked. Check with your career center to see if they sponsor specialized training for these types of interviews. The general interview guidelines in this chapter will help you with many of the questions you might face, but not all. Check out these excellent online resources to learn more about interviewing for these fields.

Financial Careers

Banks, insurance companies, and investment firms often hire financial analysts directly from on-campus recruiting and career fairs, so if you are looking for careers in this area, you will likely encounter interview questions beyond the usual "Why are you interested in our organization?" or "Why do you want to work as a financial analyst?" You will be asked behavioral questions for which the STAR technique mentioned on page 183 will be helpful.

- Tell me about a time you managed a team.
- Tell me about a time you developed a strategy for improving a situation.
- Give me an example of a complex problem you solved.
- Give me an example of a challenging project you managed.

You will also likely be asked technical questions and those are more difficult to prepare for. But knowing to expect those questions can help you prepare. For more information, check out these resources.

- **Online guide to investment banking interviews from Street of Walls (http://www.streetofwalls.com):** http://www.streetofwalls .com/finance-training-courses/investment-banking-overview-and- behavioral-training/investment-banking-job-interview

- **Career consultant Jeremy Hopkins provides sample questions and answers on his website:** https://financialanalystinterview questions.com/financial-analyst-interview-guide-one-of-a-kind-e-book

Consulting Careers

For consulting interviews, you will want to decide on the type of consulting position you're seeking and which organizations offer that type of consulting. In the area of management consulting, for example, you might be looking at business strategy, human resources, financial, or risk and compliance consulting, just to name a few. You could also be looking at environmental or IT/software, or sales consulting, so be sure you know exactly what type of consulting position you are seeking so that you don't interview for the wrong position. Case interviews are very common in consulting and require you to analyze a situation. To learn more about succeeding in a consulting interview, check out these resources.

- **Ace the Case:** http://www.acethecase.com/caseinterview
- **Management Consulted:** https://managementconsulted.com/consulting-interviews/4-types-consultant-fit-interview-questions
- **Vault guides to consulting interviews:** https://www.vault.com/blogs/interviewing/26-interview-questions-the-top-10-consulting-firms-ask
- **Street of Walls consulting interview questions and answers:** http://www.streetofwalls.com/finance-training-courses/consulting-interview-training/consulting-interview-questions

Please note some of these sites offer guidance or support for a fee. This is not an endorsement of their services. Always investigate any opportunities before paying a fee for a service. Also, check in with your career center. They (or your library) may have already purchased Vault guide or similar resources.

PART 3

Land

Find a Destination That Fits

This section will help you land safely and securely in a future that fits.

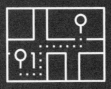

CHAPTER 9

Land a Job and Start Your Career

Does it feel like everything you've done has led you to this chapter? It was all about getting a job, right? And if you've followed the system so far, you might not even need this chapter because a job has already appeared.

Or maybe you've skipped the bulk of the chapters and jumped to this one because, well, you want a job. To make the most of this chapter and the Parachute System, however, you need to slow down for a moment. Let's take stock of where you are.

In order to find your job (your dream job, or just the job you can get at the moment, or the job that might lead you to the dream job), you need to make sure your Backpack is full. There's no point in parachuting into a location without the proper preparation and equipment. Remember, the whole point of the Parachute System is that you are in charge of the search, not the job market. If you came to this chapter to simply learn "what's out there" you are allowing the market to determine your future.

How to Proceed: The Parachute System

So how does the Parachute System help you now? Here's how it works:

1 Identify your skills, interests, knowledge, and values, and what you have to offer a potential employer or graduate school (chapters 2 and 3).

2 Identify the career fields you want to explore further. Perhaps you have a job title in mind (chapter 5).

3 Keep it simple by summarizing all the above key elements into one diagram—your Backpack for the trip. You can also fill out the "Job Search Preparation Form" on page 194 to get all your information onto one page. (See how much of the job search form you can complete. If you have gaps, you might want to consider returning to the earlier chapters and doing the exercises.)

4 Create a list of leads based on what you know about yourself and the job market.

  Gather information (research) by reading everything you can find online about your potential career(s). Learn what the typical job titles and salaries are, what the job growth predictors say, and where the bulk of the jobs are located. Learn about the culture of the industry and what the educational requirements are. In short, become an expert in the industry and jobs you are seeking.

  Then become an expert in specific companies or organizations that might hire you. Through reading job listings online, using your career center's resources (such as Vault guides) or Career*Shift*, (https://www.careershift.com), and using LinkedIn and other social media, learn everything you can about specific employers.

  As you research, simultaneously start identifying people who can help you in your search. This will include your network of family and friends, professors, college administrators, former employers, alumni, recruiters you have met, and LinkedIn or other social media connections. Your search is ultimately for someone who can directly connect you to your desired organization or job.

5 Prepare your targeted job search materials (resume, social media profiles, and so on) based on your research and knowledge of the field (chapters 6 and 7).

6 Prepare strong stories that highlight your strengths and responses to typical interview questions (chapter 8).

7 Continually try out potential careers to see if they fit you, by acquiring experiences through micro-internships, internships, summer jobs, and shadowing experiences (chapter 10).

8 Continue to build conversations with your network and approach potential employers through a variety of methods, including online applications, networking, and social media (chapter 8).

9 Consider offers and negotiate a salary.

10 Start your new career!

This whole process can seem a little daunting if you're just starting out. But you can do this at your own pace and on your own schedule, based on where you are in college at the moment. You can proceed through this a chapter at a time, if you haven't already completed the previous chapters. And the truth is, there are people who have completed the whole book in a weekend by doing a "boot camp" and focusing on nothing but their career search.

So let's start with where you need to be right now.

Job Search Preparation Form

Write down the key industries you are most interested in:

1 _____

2 _____

3 _____

Write down the job titles you want to pursue:

1 _____

2 _____

3 _____

Write down the skills you plan to focus on related to your career choices:

1 _____

2 _____

3 _____

Write down your interests that will be helpful in your career choices:

1 _____

2 _____

3 _____

Write down the values that are important to you that will align with your career choices:

1 _____

2 _____

3 _____

Name the geographic areas where you'd like to live:

1 _____

2 _____

3 _____

Name the salary range you can consider: _____

Name ten specific organizations that might hire you:

1 _____

2 _____

3 _____

4 _____

5 _____

6 _____

7 _____

8 _____

9 _____

10 _____

continued →

Job Search Preparation Form (continued)

Name key individuals in your network (alumni, friends, LinkedIn connections, etc.) who can help connect you to these organizations of this career field:

_____

_____

_____

How did you do with filling out the form? Were you able to identify everything requested? If not, then you know what gaps you need to fill in. The other chapters in this book can help you with every aspect of the form. And guess what, this form is really your Backpack—everything you need to move forward. Assuming you've filled it in completely, you can now use it as your template against which you will evaluate every opportunity you receive. If you're struggling to choose between two job offers (wouldn't that be wonderful!), you can compare them to your list of desired job characteristics and determine which would be the likely best fit for you.

It's worth looking at the chart on page 127 again, now that you've completed the Job Search Preparation Form. You might have identified all the potential leads for your field, but you might still have some prep work to do first. Take look at the chart and ask yourself the simple question, "Can I do this tomorrow?"

For instance, let's say you indicated you could do the job you're considering tomorrow.

- How do you know this?
- What information tells you that you can do it? Have you done enough information interviews to verify your opinions?
- Do you have your targeted job search materials ready? Is your social media updated?
- Have you acquired enough experience through internships, for example, that you can do it?
- What's your next action step? Are you going to pursue it now or do you have a target date for starting your search in earnest?

Getting Started in a New Geographic Location

Are you trying to start your career in a new location after graduation? You will need to prepare more carefully for your move. Consider these factors as you make your plans:

- Keep in mind you don't always have to move to a large city to start your career. Many medium-size cities are more livable and less expensive. Read the various guides to "best cities," keeping an eye on the job market. You can research the number of people your age, which might make a location more appealing. If there's a good university in the smaller city, that's often a plus. You might be able to get a graduate degree or take advantage of interesting speakers and arts- or sports-related events.

- If you're still determined to move to that expensive big city, you can always build up your resume so that when you apply for that big-city job you will be ready for a management or higher-level position that will pay more and make city life more affordable.

- Be sure to research the commute time to your new position from wherever you might be living. Some cities are known for terrible commutes (Los Angeles, Atlanta, and others), so you will want to know what public transportation options might be available. You'll need to factor commute time into your work schedule. An eight-hour day can quickly become a ten-hour day if your commute is bad. This may influence your decision on not only where to live but whether you can take the job at all.

- Entry-level positions usually don't pay relocation costs, but you can always ask.

- Some large employers (like universities, for example) will keep a list of available apartments. They might even have a discount for new employees. Always ask the human resources office about this. The list might be on a protected part of the website that you can't see.

- Is there someone you can stay with for a few weeks until you find an apartment or a more permanent place to live? A former room-mate? A relative? A friend of a friend? Ask your friends if they know anyone in your new city.

continued →

- If you do find a friend or relative who offers you temporary housing, don't wear out your welcome. Plan to stay only a week or two at most unless there is a monetary arrangement.

- Consider looking for an inexpensive Airbnb or similar opportunity. Some cities have "executive stay" hotels that rent by the week or month. They are cheaper than regular hotel rooms but probably too expensive to use for more than a month or so.

- Check Craigslist (be careful for scams!) or other city-based sites for roommate openings. If you know someone who lives in your desired location ask them to use the Nextdoor app to put a request out for you. Often people are interested in renting out a room for a short time, but they might not advertise it widely. Sites, like Nextdoor, where people generally trust the others using the site might have openings you wouldn't otherwise hear about.

The Traditional Approach, On-Campus Recruiting, and The Parachute Approach

When college students (and their parents) start thinking about the job search, one of the first places they look is the on-campus recruiting program. Many excellent employers come on campus to do one-on-one interviews, staff a career fair, offer information sessions, or otherwise make themselves known and available to students. Many employers also conduct virtual interviews and virtual information sessions through the career center. And on-campus recruiting is a great approach—for some students. But it also reinforces a major approach to the job search that won't work for many students now or after college. This approach was called "the traditional approach" by Richard Bolles.

Let's take a look at the **traditional approach** (which works sometimes—which is why it is traditional) and how it applies to on-campus recruiting and your job search. Here's the traditional approach for most job seekers, whether they are college students or not:

1   You start with the job market. You read the articles about what's hot and what's lucrative and you pick one of those fields.
2   You look at the jobs online for that field.
3   You write a resume and cover letter and you put in a bunch of applications. And I do mean a bunch. Like maybe one hundred. And then you wait.
4   If that doesn't work, you look online again and you apply again.
5   Repeat until something happens.

But Richard Bolles discovered a secret about the traditional approach: it doesn't work, at least not for a majority of people. It's fine if you are so highly desired in the market, and your skillset is so needed, that employers are looking for you. And it can sometimes work if you have a specific identified talent, and you apply to a specific place that hires your specific talent.

So there's a reason it's traditional, and it continues to hang around—it sometimes works. Many computer science and engineering majors have found that the traditional approach works just fine for their careers. So if you fit into that group of people who are highly sought after in a limited market, and it works for you, great. Just don't count on it.

Here's the **on campus recruiting** version of the traditional approach:

1 You look at the employers coming to campus or interviewing virtually.
2 You adjust your resume to fit one of the career fields associated with your career center and apply.
3 Your GPA, major, and experiences fit what the employers are seeking, so they select you for an interview.
4 You interview successfully.
5 They invite you to a site interview at their organization.
6 They offer you a job and you take it.

That's the dream for a lot of college students and here's why:

- On-campus recruiting is convenient and relatively easy. They are almost literally at your door, and they are hiring college students.

- The process is much simpler and more transparent than the job search you would do off-campus. You review the opportunities coming to your campus, select a few that sound the most interesting or promising, put in your resume, and wait and see.

- You don't have to really think too hard about what you want—the employers are telling you what they want.

- You feel a great degree of satisfaction because you feel in charge of your search. You're taking action.

- You're staying in line with what your friends are doing—maybe you even feel a little superior because you're moving much more quickly to your future than your friends seem to be.

- You can see this amazing path to your future in a well-respected and well-paying, career field.

On-campus interviewing, whether in person or virtual, is wonderful. Where else will you have a chance to meet with so many employers who are eager to hire you? Some of the best corporations in the nation are likely coming to your campus, and many offer well-designed training programs and special opportunities for recent college graduates. So if you fit the mold of on-campus recruiting, by all means use it.

But there's another side to on-campus recruiting you might not be aware of. On-campus recruiting is kind of like a lottery approach to the job market. Only a certain number of students will win because:

- The same students compete for the same jobs. This means you are always competing directly with the same students in your major and class year who might have higher GPAs or might have more experience.

- The numbers simply work against you. An employer might present an information session to fifty students. Then they will select twelve students they will interview during a day on campus. Finally they will extend an offer to two, possibly three, students, at most. While those numbers shouldn't scare you away, they do serve as a realistic reminder that recruiting isn't the sure thing you might think it is.

- On-campus recruiting gives you a highly skewed perspective on the job market—coloring your view of what's out there. (Many students express an interest in consulting without knowing much about it. All they know is that consulting firms show up on campus every year.)

- Many employers and career fields are not represented on-campus due to everything from small budgets that don't allow them to travel to only having a few positions open, making a broad search unnecessary. The types of industries that hire a lot of young people just out of college—banking/finance, retail, insurance, consulting, and so on—are over-represented, while the smaller industries are under-represented. The arts, nonprofit organizations, business specialties, like public relations or human resources, among others, are not well represented with on-campus recruiting. (This is not the fault of your career center, by the way. This is a factor of the job market in general.)

- On-campus recruiting can make you feel left out because your major isn't popular with the employers. Many students report feelings of depression and anxiety when they don't have the same access to their desired career fields as students who are seeking a traditional business or tech career.

- It creates an understandable resentment among students who either aren't interested in the employers who come to campus or who see their friends have an easy entry into the job market while they have to work much harder to find their spot. And there's some truth in that.

- Some students report buyer's remorse after taking an offer from a company. They are so caught up in the recruiting drama and pressure, they stop thinking about what they really want. Alumni often return to their career center regretting that they didn't explore the job market more thoroughly when they were a student.

So overall there are some problems associated with on-campus recruiting. You might not fit the exact qualifications the employer is seeking and get shut out of the system. You might be focusing your career aspirations on a highly limited number of potential options. You might be more focused on who might want you rather than what you want?

But that's why the Parachute System is here for you. You are going to create your own safe place to land into the market. And you aren't doing it alone. You have this book. And you have a career center.

Believe it or not, career centers are interested in all careers. Not just the ones that recruit on campus. They believe in you and your search, and they want to help. That doesn't mean they are always well-staffed or funded by the university. I have worked with literally thousands of career professionals at career centers across the country, and I have never met one who wasn't concerned with *all* their students' career paths. They care, and they want to help, so take advantage of that.

By all means, take advantage of any employer who fits your plans if representatives come to your campus. Go to the career fairs and apply for any positions that interest you. On-campus recruiting is a great way to learn more about how the job search process works. You can practice your interviewing skills and learn about jobs and opportunities you might not otherwise have considered.

But let's step away from on-campus recruiting (and the traditional mindset it reinforces) and compare what Bolles called the "Traditional Search" with the **Parachute Approach** you're learning:

- You're not just looking for a job . . . you're looking for an **ideal job that uses your skills and knowledge**.
- You're not just waiting to see which employers show up . . . you're finding interesting openings and **designing your own path**.
- You're not focusing on the hot jobs or what others are doing . . . you're focused on **what works and fits for you**.
- You're not just using the on-campus interviewing process . . . you're **actively talking to alumni and potential employers** about what you want.
- You're not just writing a resume and posting on some online site . . . you're **using LinkedIn and other social media to start conversations** that will lead to opportunities.

- You're exploring the best ways to **get the attention of recruiters and hiring managers.**
- You're focusing on yourself and what you want. You're **not comparing yourself to others** in this process.
- You are **moving forward with confidence** and taking actions even if you don't know if they will succeed.
- You don't let a less-than-perfect experience keep you stuck. You **constantly look for what's next.**
- You apply to opportunities even if you don't match every job requirement. You **look for opportunities** where one or two of your skills can shine.

Do you see the difference? Can you feel the shift from "I'm basically helpless and have to just hope some employer shows up on campus" to "I'm in charge of my future." Yes, it's more work, but that's short-term thinking. Focus on the end game, the future that's more aligned, the future that fits.

By this time you should have a strong sense of how to proceed in your search for a job, and you're ready to get started. Don't forget to keep "you" as your focus throughout the search. As you research your field and come up with responses to interview questions, make them personal, not generic. Why do *you* want this career? This industry? This job? What will it mean for you? Make sure your answers are interesting and reveal more about you and the work you have done to get to this point.

You are always on the lookout for the next great career idea or connection, so if you see something interesting, go for it! Maybe you see a poster in your department for an upcoming speaker. Maybe your friends are always going to a particular club or organization, check it out. Be open to experiences—you never know where they will lead.

Schedule time to work on your future. Whether that is to work on the exercises in this book, visit your career center, or write your resume, most career-related activities won't happen by chance. You will need to schedule them into your daily or weekly plans. Even if you can only give yourself thirty minutes to devote to career activities, that's enough to get started. In thirty minutes, you can do an internet search, locate and contact one alumnus, and sign up for a career coaching appointment. You can accomplish a lot in just a few minutes if you focus.

Look for career-related emails, podcasts, and newsletters you can subscribe to. Even if you don't have time to read or listen to everything, the regular stream of items in your email will remind you about your job goals on a regular basis. Set a Google alert for your specific field. Don't

From Commitment to Career

After doing the exercises in the first section of this book, Matt realized that his primary goal was to find a career that matched his strong value system. And for Matt, his commitment to a sustainable environment superseded all other interests. He realized that his career needed to be related to sustainability.

He began researching the field and quickly learned that there are three main perspectives on sustainability: business management, science/technology, and public policy. They intersect in some careers, but they have a slightly different focus with the business side focusing mainly on profit, the science focusing on environmental protections, and the policy side focusing on social responsibility. He realized that he could envision the different areas this way, envisioning possible overlaps between the different specialties.

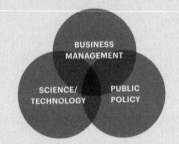

Matt searched the job placement records of various colleges offering degrees in sustainability as well as Indeed.com and found a variety of job titles within the field.

Administrative services manager	Analyst, corporate sustainability
Chemist	Climate change analyst
Community services manager	Conservation scientist
Corporate sustainability professor	Corporate sustainability strategist
Culture engagement manager	Director of sustainability
Energy consultant	Environmental attorney
Environmental engineer	Environmental specialist
Environmental sustainability planner	Financial analyst
Graphic designer	Intern, sustainability manufacturing and sourcing

Manager, sustainability consulting business	Product manager for sustainability
Public relations specialist	Risk management specialist
Science teacher	Sustainability consultant
Sustainability specialist	Urban planner

One of the things he noticed as he compiled his list was that in many cases the positions did not require a sustainability degree; they were general positions that focused on sustainability within an organization. For instance, graphic designers and public relations specialists can be found in a variety of fields; but in this case, the positions were specifically located in settings where the focus was sustainability.

Companies posting sustainability positions included local, state, and federal governments; major medical centers; and corporations, like Nike, Starbucks, and Kimberly-Clark. He also learned that a variety of majors (such as the following) can lead to a sustainability career.

Anthropology	Biology
Business, with a concentration in sustainability	Engineering science
Environmental engineering	Environmental law and policy
Environmental science	Environmental studies
Forestry	Geology
Marine biology/oceanography	Natural resource management
Political science	Public policy
Sociology	Sustainable agriculture

Matt quickly realized that he can pursue almost any career and still have a sustainability focus, depending on the organization for which he works. He focused on the questions he answered in chapter 2 and created this chart to focus his interests related to sustainability:

What would I like to change?	What are the challenges?
Focus on factors that are valuable to business (profit, savings) that also support the environment. Create business strategies that are more ethical and social. Help organizations see the long-term value of sustainability efforts.	Finding a company that sincerely wants to make changes. Finding an industry where I could specialize in sustainability and use my other skills and knowledge in my career. Need to decide on the industries that most interest me.

continued →

What would I like to improve?

Our environmental footprint. I'd like to find an industry that is currently not as sustainable as it could be and be part of the change.

What are the opportunities?

Pretty much unlimited if I stay open to the possibilities. Since starting my research, I have already found one company near my home, so I'm going to see if an alumnus from my school works there and set up a phone call. If possible I'd like to visit the company.

He is currently a business major, and based on his skills and knowledge, he has decided to lean toward the business end of sustainability and seek positions in corporations that are focusing on improving their sustainability.

He developed an Excel spreadsheet listing potential employers, including organizations he finds on Indeed, through his alumni resources at his university, and through some of the following job listing sites.

- **SustainableBusiness.com:** https://www.sustainablebusiness.com/greendreamjobs/jobs
- **GreenBiz:** http://jobs.greenbiz.com
- **Idealist:** https://www.idealist.org/en

Through his extensive research, he found a site called Corporate Knights that focuses on the companies that are doing something right related to sustainability. One of the top 100 companies is McCormick & Co., which just happens to be located near his home in Baltimore. Reading their website, he learned they are committed to community and environment. Since he will be going home in a few weeks for winter break, his next step is to go on LinkedIn to see if any alumni from his school are working there. If they are, he will reach out to them and see if he can arrange a visit to the company over his break. If he can't find any alumni, he will reach out to someone who has a job title that fits his area of interest to see if they are willing to take a phone call. During that phone call, he will try to arrange a visit to the company over his break. He's excited about finding an opportunity that not only fits his career plans, but is located close to his home and family.

be too general; for instance a Google alert for "psychology jobs" would quickly fill your inbox, but an alert for "child development specialist jobs" would yield more targeted results.

Always check with your career center to see if they have purchased industry guides, like Vault, or other types of programs that help you analyze careers. Not every center can afford those products, but there are some excellent free online resources where you can learn a lot. Two of the best research tools for careers are free and available to everyone: the Occupational Outlook Handbook (https://www.bls.gov/ooh) and the O*NET (https://www.onetonline.org).

Keep going. Always be connecting. And always be thankful. If someone takes the time to speak with you or help you in any way, always send a thank-you email or note. So few people do, and you will be remembered in a positive way.

Managing the Job Offer

So you've followed this system and—it worked! You have a job offer. Now what?

Take a moment to celebrate, even if it's just a quick happy dance in your room. Then, think about your next steps. How do you feel about this offer? Is it *the* job, the one you've been dreaming of? Or is it an okay job, one that's sort of interesting but not the best? You'll need to make a decision, and that can be hard. One major factor in your decision will need to be the job market. What is the employment picture generally? Is this a good market where you can hold out for a better offer, or are you in a situation where you need to take an offer rather than let it go. Think back to the "perfect" job you created in the early chapters of this book. How close does this opportunity resemble that? If it doesn't fit exactly (and many jobs won't) is it close? Is it a stepping-stone job to the opportunity you really want? Will it boost your resume and add something that will be helpful later? These are all considerations as you decide whether to accept the job or not. You can always talk to your family, the career center, your professors, and others if outside opinions might be helpful.

What you don't want to do is accept the offer, so you'll have a "safety" employer, and then keep looking for other jobs. You don't want to ultimately renege on the offer. It is highly unethical to accept a job offer and then rescind the acceptance later. It's much better to say no and keep looking if the offer isn't what you want. If you know you don't want the position, simply reply to the email or call, indicating that while you greatly appreciated the interview process and you enjoyed meeting them, this position is not right for you at the present time. Be pleasant and appreciative—you never know when or if you might encounter that company or that person again. Human resources staff move around from company to company, and they will remember you if you withdraw your acceptance.

But let's assume that you do want to take the offer. Let's go back to that original notification that had you doing your happy dance. How did you find out about the offer? Was it an email or a phone message? If that's the case, write down what was stated in the phone message or carefully reread the email.

A bonafide job offer will include a title, a starting date, a salary, and a reference to benefits. If you're missing any of that information, follow up with questions. If the offer was made over the phone, ask to have it in writing. Until you have something in writing, you don't have an official offer to respond to. If they send you a contract, always read it thoroughly before signing. Don't assume that "it will be fine."

Regardless of how you were informed, if you are considering the offer, follow up immediately with a phone call or reply to the email. Be gracious and indicate that you are quite pleased to receive the offer. Ask when they would like your answer. If possible, see if you can get at least a day or two to consider it. Try not to accept the offer immediately, even if it's the job you've been waiting for. You want to make sure you know all the details before you officially accept it.

Most employers will allow you to take a few days to consider the offer. (In fact, be careful of "exploding" offers that put you under a tight constraint. You can get locked into something before you're ready.)

Now that you have an offer, it's time to learn as much as you can before you say yes. Ask about the benefits package. You might be able to find some information on the company website, but it might be password-protected. Ask if you can speak with someone in the benefits office to learn more if needed. Consider asking for a flow chart of the office in which you'll be working so you will know who you would be reporting to and how your position fits in the overall office scheme. You can also ask who your contact person should be if you have more questions. Some companies have onboarding services that might include assistance with finding a place to live or discounts on moving companies, apartment rentals, and so on. Inquire about that if you need the assistance. Keep in mind while you are doing this to be pleasant and polite. If they don't have a service, move on to the next question.

A common concern among college students is whether to negotiate an offer. It depends. Some experts say you should always negotiate. But negotiating is more common when you have worked for a few years and have direct experience to offer. If you're hiring into a highly competitive field (like computer programming) you might have a better chance with negotiating than if you are entering a general management program with a lot of other new college graduates. Also, consider the job market generally and the unemployment rate. When the unemployment rate is high, it's often harder to negotiate because employers can find other workers. If the job market is strong, however, your potential for successfully negotiating a higher salary is better.

Before automatically trying to negotiate, consider whether the salary offered is fair. Consider the geographic area in which the position is located—is the salary too low to cover the cost of rent? That might be a reasonable justification for asking for a higher starting salary. But is it close to what you were hoping to get, or even a little higher? Is it the job you've been wanting? Certainly, if you're pleased with the offer, there's no need to negotiate.

If salary isn't the issue, are there other things you should negotiate instead? Investigate the benefits package and see if anything there could or should be negotiated. Maybe you can request a different title. Do you need to adjust the starting date? For instance, let's say they want you to start working on August 1, and you won't start accruing vacation time until September 1. But you're committed to being in a friend's wedding and need to take a mid-August Friday off in order to get to the wedding. That's an item to negotiate. Don't wait until you show up the first day on the job and then announce you'll be out on a Friday two weeks from then. Negotiate this ahead of time. (Worst case scenario: they say no to taking the Friday off. Well, now you have more negotiating to do, such as a later starting date so you can be in your friend's wedding. Or you might have to alter your travel plans so you can work on that Friday.)

Once you believe you have the necessary information to make the right decision, by all means accept the offer. And breathe a huge sigh of relief. You did it! Congratulations!

What If You Don't Hear Anything?

What if after all this work and interviewing, you don't hear anything from the employers?

Give the process a week or two after your interview before following up. Hopefully, you asked at your last interview what the timeline was for hearing about the decision. Respect what you were told. If you were told it would be two weeks, wait at least two weeks before you contact them (other than sending your thank-you note). Filling positions often takes longer than planned at many organizations. The delay in responding to you may have nothing to do with you or their ultimate decision. Their process may simply have been delayed.

You can follow up with any employer you haven't heard from by sending an email. Keep the tone pleasant and simply write something like "I just wanted to thank you again for interviewing me last week for the position of _____. I greatly enjoyed our interview, and I was wondering if there are any updates to the hiring process?" (If something good has happened since you last interacted with them—you graduated or learned that you're getting an honor—you can mention that update in your email.) "I am still very interested in the position, and I hope to hear from you soon."

If you don't get a response to your follow-up email, move on to another opportunity. For legal reasons, some companies do not engage in emails with individuals they are not hiring. You can always follow-up again a few months later if you're still looking and want to know if any new opportunities have come up.

But it's best to move on if the organization isn't reaching out. Just set your sights on another opportunity.

CHAPTER 10

Land an Internship or Short-Term Experience

Despite all you are learning in the classroom, gaining real world experience through internships and other activities will greatly improve your chances in the job market. Employers want to see proof of your ability to perform the skills you say you have in your resume or on your social media profile, and an internship or other work experience is the best way to demonstrate this. Acquiring experience can also counter a low GPA. In this chapter we're going to focus on finding short-term experiences that will build your knowledge and develop new skills and competencies. Lots of activities fall into this category: volunteering, summer jobs, shadowing experiences, micro-internships, practicums, setting up your own business, and internships.

• • •

Alex planned to return home from his first year in college and find an internship in a finance-related field. Everyone, even his parents, said that getting an internship was not just important but imperative—"you must have internships on your resume." But he had already checked with the two banks in his small town and neither had any openings. After realizing his hometown wasn't going to provide an internship, Alex went to the career center for help, only to learn that most of the finance internships they advertised were for sophomores and juniors. Alex was frustrated and stressed. How could he get experience when every opportunity required experience?

• • •

Chances are, like Alex, you've been hearing about internships ever since you got to campus. And, like Alex, you're probably getting stressed if you haven't found one. Or perhaps you can't afford one because internships in your field of interest don't pay, and you need the income. Taking a free internship is a luxury you can't afford. Or the best internships are located in major cities, and you don't have an inexpensive way to live there.

It's true that internships are an excellent way to acquire experience— and experience does rule in the job search. Employers are always seeking candidates who are career-ready, meaning that they have the skills and experience to do the job quickly. They can be excellent ways to demonstrate that you have those requisite skills. And internships look great on your resume because they demonstrate commitment to a career and show that you have the specific knowledge and experience for your field. Through an internship, you can develop transferable skills that can benefit you in any employment situation. Internships can clarify your career plans by helping you decide whether the career field you desire is really that desirable. And because they are often prestigious, they offer a powerful way into a professional position, and can pay more than a traditional summer job, it's no surprise that the best internships can be highly competitive and difficult to obtain.

However, as mentioned, not all internships are paid, so doing an internship might not be an option for you. And not every internship is a valuable experience. Much of the work can be boring or uninteresting ("get my coffee, please"). One intern at a prestigious consulting firm spent much of her summer inventorying the supply closet because her site didn't secure an expected contract that would have had work for her. So an internship isn't always the best choice for your career plans.

Get rid of this notion that you *must* have an internship. Yes, internships are helpful. Yes, employers often hire from internships. But not everyone can get an internship for a lot of reasons. And it's okay. There's a difference between what is desirable and what is necessary. Internships are desirable, experience is necessary. So let's think more broadly about how to acquire experience rather than worrying too much about the label of "internship."

The bottom line: your overarching goals are to learn, acquire experience, and make potential connections for your future. You are just as likely to do that in another short-term experience, such as a part-time job, a summer job, or a volunteer experience. And whether you are paid or not doesn't change the value of the experience.

What do you hope to gain from the experience? As you consider internships and other short-term experiences, focus on your personal goals.

- **Earn income?** You'll need to research your best option for this. Some internships are paid but many are not. You might need to take a less-than-glamorous summer job instead. Or, if you do an unpaid internship and need income, you might also need to work a part-time job. If the only jobs you can find in your summer location are basic lifeguard/babysitting/fast food/retail positions—take one! Yes, they are career-builders even though they don't seem like it. You can build your understanding of how workplaces function through these jobs—and you never know what connections you might make if you're friendly to the customers. Many a Starbucks barista has found connections through providing coffee every morning to someone in their desired profession.

- **Build skills?** Here you're not only thinking about direct skills that relate to your future employment but also acquiring transferable skills, like general office-work skills, or specific skills, like computer software or data analysis. You will also build your soft skills of working with a team, learning to handle difficult office relationships, or getting along with a supervisor. You will learn about the culture and the unwritten rules of the workplace and observe "meeting behavior" and office interactions—all valuable skills for your future.

- **Build knowledge?** Be creative when seeking ways to improve your knowledge. Can you find a volunteer opportunity that will allow you to learn or work with clients or a community issue that interests you? What about online learning? Would a Skillshare or Udemy course, or YouTube videos, teach you what you need to know? Maybe a community college class could help? Take advantage of the extra free time in the summer away from the traditional classroom to create your own learning experience.

- **Learn project and time management?** In any workplace, volunteer or paid, projects happen quickly. You won't have all semester to write a report—you'll have a day in some cases. So you will learn to manage your time and keep up with several projects at once. You'll learn to set goals and deadlines. These are invaluable skills that will help you throughout your career.

- **Build connections?** In some industries, like consulting and finance, internships can be the main ticket into a full-time job with a prestigious organization. If you do well, you are likely to receive an offer to return. But any experience can help you build your connections if you do a good job and receive strong recommendations. You never know who might be able to connect you to a valuable network, so never hesitate to ask your colleagues and supervisors for suggestions for building your network. Develop a network of connections no matter what the setting.

- **Acquire direct experience in a desired career field?** Finding any experience (internship, volunteer, part-time job) that places you in your desired career field is like finding a vein of gold. You can tap this experience for so much learning and knowledge. You will greatly improve the stories you can tell a potential employer, and your resume will stand out.

- **Clarify career plans?** Getting into an environment that gives you a feel for your future career is invaluable. For instance, you may know you want to be a teacher, but doing an internship or other experience might help you determine a specific niche or area of specialization. And now you'll be able to have the experience to back up your job or graduate school application.

How to Find an Internship or Other Short-Term Experience

To start your internship search process, take a moment to identify the knowledge and skills you want to acquire. Remember the Knowledge Inventory you created in chapter 3 (page 71)? Try creating a similar one to identify the type of internship experience you might want to have and how to attain it.

MY STRENGTHS AND WHAT I CAN CONTRIBUTE:	WHAT I WANT TO LEARN:	WHERE COULD I LEARN THIS?

WHO CAN HELP?	HOW TO SET IT UP?

Now that you've clarified what you hope to learn, the Parachute System is a great way to find and apply for an internship, volunteer opportunity, or summer job. You're already ahead of the game because you have completed the exercises in the first four chapters. The second section of the book helped you get ready for any potential interviews, write your cover letter and resume, fill out applications, and create your social media profile. All these activities will help you connect to your next experience.

And as you think about seeking or creating these unique opportunities, look for ways to incorporate your experience gathering into your school schedule. Consider seeking fall and spring opportunities on or near your campus. Some on-campus jobs can be great pre-professional experiences. See if you can create a course schedule that leaves blocks of time open on Fridays, or an afternoon or two a week. That might just be enough to work as an intern, particularly if some of the work is virtual so you could do it in the evenings or on weekends. Following are some steps you can take to enhance your search for experience.

Learn about Your School's Internship Policies and Opportunities

- Check with your college regarding any regulations around internships.
- Is there an internship office you can visit? Or are internships handled in academic departments or through the career center?
- Does your school offer credit for internships? If the internship is in the summer, is there a reduced-tuition option?
- Does your school have any requirements around whether internships for credit are paid or unpaid?
- Check your academic department to see if they list internships for students.

- Frequently check your career center's job board to see if any internships are listed.
- Even if you're not doing your internship for credit, see if your school has a learning contract for those who are doing an internship for credit. You can create your own learning contract and share it with your employer. This might encourage an employer to take a chance on you, even if they don't normally offer internships.

So how do you find that perfect internship?

The most important thing you can do is start early. Many of the best internships can take a year to apply/obtain. Investment banking, consulting, and prestigious federal agencies (FBI and CIA, among many) offer great internship opportunities, but you must apply early. The minute you know the career field you're seeking, start investigating opportunities. Even if internships are reserved for juniors, for example, companies often start the interviewing process a year, sometimes eighteen months ahead(!). Some positions require security or background checks, which also slows the process.

The best place to begin your search is at your career center. Their website and job database will likely have local as well as national opportunities. Many of the companies that come to campus for job interviews also have internship opportunities. Sometimes your career center or alumni office will post internship opportunities from alumni. Attend any career fairs, networking events, or workshops your career center offers. Even at job fairs, many employers are also seeking interns. You might also discover great researching resources, like Vault guides or Career*Shift*.

Check out the career center websites at other colleges for internship listings. Think about the geographic areas where you would like to intern and note any nearby colleges and universities. Many internships are advertised locally so you might have better results if you search sites that cater to the local area. For example, if you want to intern in the northern California area, check out CalBerkeley's career center website page for internship information: https://career.berkeley.edu/Internships/Internships. Some of the information is protected for their students only, but there are a variety of links you'll be able to follow to learn more about regional opportunities.

In addition to checking out your career center, talk to everyone you know. Speak with family, friends, faculty, college advisors, and career counselors. If you have the opportunity to speak with someone who works at a company or organization you're interested in, propose an internship to them. Review your strengths and let them know you're offering them your time, your skills, and education.

If your career center doesn't offer alumni connections, contact your college or university alumni office to connect with alumni who are working in your field of interest. The purpose of this initial contact is not to ask for an internship or job, but rather to "meet" them online, let them know of your interest in their career field, and ask if you can contact them in the future for ideas and suggestions for getting into their field of work. You are information gathering for the future, and you never know if they might have an internship opportunity for you.

Research companies that offer internships in your field of interest. Know where the opportunities might be by reading about the divisions within the company, job opening descriptions, and so on. Telephone or visit employers in your geographic and/or career areas of interest and inquire about summer jobs/internships. Just have your pitch ready (chapter 8) and make sure you have an updated resume (chapter 6).

If you're having difficulty finding internship opportunities, consider developing a small business or entrepreneurial activity that can build your skills and knowledge. What skills do you have that someone might pay for? Can you help a local entrepreneur develop their social media plan? Can you design a website for a new author? Can you add extra jobs (like babysitting or yardwork) to your schedule? Develop an online course and teach others a skill you have? Nothing impresses employers like a hard worker—and while everyone says they are a hard worker, you will be able to prove it.

Keep in mind that not all internships are in physical locations. Consider an online internship or a micro-internship. Micro-internships are short projects that need to be completed within a specific time frame. Micro-internships are a great way to add value to your resume and demonstrate your skills. They can serve as an entry into the organization. Through Parker-Dewey (https://www.parkerdewey.com) you can be paid anywhere from $200 to $600 and complete the project in the comfort of your dorm room or library. Online and micro-internships are great resources for student athletes and other students who don't have time for a traditional internship. Check out Intern Queen (https://www.intern queen.com) and Lauren Berger's LinkedIn (https://careers.linkedin.com/ students/Internships) to find out more about online internships. For paid short-term jobs, check out Coolworks (https://www.coolworks.com).

Although the internet is a great place to start learning about already established internships, try to avoid using it to apply for internships. If you find an internship you're really interested in, by all means apply online if the website offers that, but your next step should be to see if you can make an in-person connection. This is where you'll want to use those networking skills you learned in chapter 8. Just know that lots of people are using the same resources, so if you can find a more direct or personal way to network or connect, do that. Here are some other resources.

INTERNSHIP SITE	URL
Chegg Internships	https://www.internships.com
Craigslist	https://Craigslist.org (Then enter the geographic area where you want to intern.) Be careful—scams are common. Do not send any funds or personal information until you can verify the opportunity.
FindSpark	https://www.findspark.com
Glassdoor	https://www.glassdoor.com/Students/index.htm
Goabroad	https://www.goabroad.com
Google	Type in your area of interest, such as "marketing internship, Atlanta, GA"
House of Representatives internships	https://www.house.gov/educators-and-students/college-internships
Idealist	https://www.idealist.org/en
Indeed	https://www.indeed.com/q-Internship-jobs.html
Internship programs	http://www.internshipprograms.com
Senate internships	https://www.senate.gov/employment/po/internships.htm
SimplyHired	https://www.simplyhired.com
Smart Intern China	http://www.smartinternchina.com
The Washington Center	http://twc.edu
USAJobs	https://www.usajobs.gov
WayUp	https://www.wayup.com
Youtern	https://www.youtern.com
Zip Recruiter	https://www.ziprecruiter.com

No Internship? Stuck in an Uninspiring Summer Job? No Worries

Even if you can't find an internship, you can craft an amazing summer experience. Remember Alex from the beginning of this chapter? Here's the rest of his story.

• • •

Instead of telling Alex that he was out of luck for this summer, his career center coach helped him do something else: construct an amazing "Summer Experience." His coach started with a simple question, "What would you like to say you have done or learned by the end of this summer?" They made a list of his learning goals for the summer and crafted a way to achieve them through reading books, connecting with finance alumni from his school, setting up information interviews with the bank managers in his town, and signing up for some basic accounting classes online through Udemy. He even did a micro-internship online. It didn't matter that his summer job was working for a landscaping business. His summer was packed with invaluable knowledge, connections, and experiences. Alex knew he would have no trouble describing his summer experience to a potential employer.

• • •

Finding ways to fill your basic need for income and creating a well-rounded summer experience will not only benefit you for future opportunities, but you will also help clarify your career plans and serve as the basis for terrific stories for future interviews.

While it would be wonderful if you could find a paying job or internship in your field of interest, it's just as likely you will need to take a summer job that simply gives you the income you need to go back to school. You might be a food server, a hotel desk clerk, a cashier, or any other typical summer or part-time job. Those jobs are fine for building basic workplace skills. You learn responsibility, customer service, and how to deal with difficult people. Never underestimate the value of work experience in general, even if it is less than glamorous. What is more important is what you choose to do to enhance your summer experience.

• • •

Hannah found a summer job at a frozen yogurt franchise. Her main duties were to open and close the store, maintain a health code–compliant serving area, greet customers, and create the different menu items. It was a basic summer job and the hourly rate was better than at other places, so it made sense for her to do this work even though it had nothing to do with her future plans. She wants to get into marketing and is particularly interested in branding. Here's how she outlined her summer plan of action:

- *Talk with the manager of the franchise. Find out who does the marketing for this frozen yogurt chain. Find out the location of the head office.*

- *See if the store manager could connect her to the district manager, who might connect her to the corporate office, where she might find someone on the marketing team.*

- *Arrange information interviews with a marketing representative to learn how they develop their ideas—what to feature, how early do they start their campaigns, and what kind of customer research do they do. How do their ideas about marketing fit with what they hear from customers?*

- *Take a look at the marketing offered by any competitors. What do they do differently? How is her product "branded" versus theirs? Which is better?*

- *After every conversation, send a thank-you email. (Do you have any idea how many summer workers actually do this? Virtually none. So you stand out now. Maybe you didn't plan a career in frozen yogurt, but in business you will find that people move around. They may have interesting connections you wouldn't suspect.)*

- *Identify three key books about marketing and plan to read one per month over the summer. Take notes on learning and the information that might be helpful in the future.*

- *Check out online short classes on Udemy or other platforms to learn the basics of marketing, sales, promotion, and branding. Again, take notes and keep any handouts the courses provide. Learn about the keywords or basic vocabulary in the field and be able to use that information in future interviews and on her resume.*

• • •

Now it's your turn. Crafting your summer experience is simple. Start by setting some goals. What would you like to say that you accomplished over the summer?

- Acquired a new skill or talent, or built up knowledge in a particular field?
- Developed a network of connections for future opportunities?
- Earned an income?

Review your Backpack Inventory. What skills do you currently have that you'd like to keep using? What skills do you need to develop for your field of interest? If you don't know what you want to do in the future, rely on the list of competencies from chapter 3. What competencies do you already have that you could offer an employer, and what competencies could you build through your short-term experience?

Answer the questions in the form on pages 222 to 223 to develop your summer experience. The purpose of this form is to help you create your own compelling summer experience that will help you clarify, enhance, and support your future plans. Through this experience, you will set your learning goals, determine the skills you want to develop, and challenge yourself to create a truly valuable and memorable summer. You get to design this experience in whatever way works best for you.

Here are some ideas for building your knowledge and skills over the summer:

- Build up your knowledge of a subject matter. Again, with extra time in the summer and no required reading for class, you can read books related to your future career field. Try a Google search of "best books for careers in ____" and see what shows up. If you don't have the funds to purchase the books, take advantage of your community library. It's likely they will have the titles in several formats, including eBooks.

- Another way to build knowledge (and your network) is to use social media to find the key players in your field. Who is active on LinkedIn, Twitter, or other social media sites? Who is writing/researching your field of interest? You can find terrific links to articles, blog posts, and podcasts through social media and Google searches. Once you've identified key players, researchers, or writers in your field, follow them. Get their emails, newsletters, or other resources (often free) that will allow you to learn more.

- Start building a list of potential contacts whom you could ask for guidance. Write questions or respond to blog posts, seeking the authors' advice. While many bloggers don't have the time to respond individually to all questions, they might be willing to answer questions posed on their blog sites, or they might even write blogs about that topic in the future.

Name: _____

Starting date: _____ Ending date: _____

The main outcome I hope to have from this summer experience is:

_____

_____

Where will I be spending my summer?

_____

_____

What is my planned source of income (if needed)?

_____

Does this income source fit my overall learning plan? If so, how?

_____

_____

If not, how will I develop it into a better experience? What benefit besides money can I acquire from it?

_____

_____

Key elements from my Backpack: _____

Skills: _____

Interests: _____

Values: _____

Career ideas: _____

What do I plan to learn?

_____

_____

What knowledge will I be acquiring?

What career field will I be researching?

How am I going to learn? Courses at other schools? Online courses? (Udemy, Coursera, Kahn Academy, etc.)

Books I plan to read: _____

Websites I will read: _____

Professional organizations related to my interest area:

What skills do I plan to acquire?

What is my elevator pitch for this experience?

What story do I hope to tell at the end of the summer?

How will I structure my time? (For example: "I plan to spend one day a week on . . ." or "I plan to write 500 words a day related to . . . ")

My level of commitment to this project is: (1= I don't think I can do this. 5= Energized. I believe this project will make a difference.)

1   2   3   4   5

Ensuring a Successful Internship

Once you've landed the internship, make the most of it to increase your chances of being invited back to a full-time position and ensure that you'll get great recommendations. Here's how.

Build Your Employer's Trust

- Show that you care through your behavior every day.

- Show up on time and don't leave early. If others are working late, offer to help.

- Learn how to do basic office tasks, like answering the phone, making photocopies, handling emails. Remember that even (especially) when you're tasked with simple things, you are being watched. If you don't do a good job with the basic tasks, you will likely not be asked to do anything more complex.

- If you discover that you're lacking knowledge of a key computer program, app, or other facet of the job, learn as quickly as possible. Ask for assistance, look up instructional videos online, or find a book that explains the concepts you might be lacking. Let your supervisor know you're learning "off the job." It never hurts to mention the additional research you're doing.

- Offer to assist with whatever projects or tasks people are working on. Check with your supervisor to see if it's all right to help others in the office.

- Always have a folder or notebook to write on and always have something to write with. Don't rely on your memory; take notes about assignments, important names, key information. Never assume you will remember—you won't.

- Make sure you keep your cell phone and computer charged.

- Stay pleasant and positive. Greet everyone regardless of title.

- Don't take company property home unless instructed to. You don't want to be responsible for losing a company's computer or the project that was stored on a thumb drive.

- Stay organized with your projects, and especially with other people's projects. Keep everything where it belongs so you can quickly respond to any requests.

- Stay busy. Take on an ongoing task, like data entry or filing, that you can always work on when you don't have other things to do.

Read the Culture and Imitate It

- Study what people are wearing and dress accordingly, within reason. No one will expect you to spend as much money on clothes as a professional. Use accessories (like ties, jewelry, or scarves) to make the same outfit look different.

- Notice factors such as name tags, use of cell phones in meetings, and the overall atmosphere.

    - Is it a friendly, chatty office? Do people just "drop-in" to chat? If not, don't be the "chatterbox" in the office.

    - Do people use email a lot? Is the tone used in emails professional or casual? Remember that even if the tone is casual, your emails should be more formal and polite initially until you know people better.

    - What about texting? Are you expected to respond after hours or on weekends?

- Stay out of office gossip and politics. It's not your business. You don't have the depth of knowledge to know why people are saying/doing what they are doing, so just observe. Avoid offering your opinion about other people if asked. Stay positive in your observations. You don't know the backstory or who might be friends with whom.

An internship serves so many purposes in preparing you for the workplace. You have the opportunity to assess a career field without committing to it, learn the "inside scoop" on what the industry and work setting is like, make potentially invaluable connections for future employment, and confirm your genuine, fact-based, realistic career choice. At the same time, do not stress if you're unable to complete an internship; there are many ways to acquire experience and an internship is just one. Remember, the ultimate goal is to learn about a career field firsthand, so that should be your focus.

Land in Graduate or Professional School

Are you thinking of going to graduate school? Or maybe a professional school such as medical or law school? Many college students do, particularly if they have done well academically and enjoy learning. Graduate study can give you an in-depth understanding of your area of interest, help prepare you for your career, and give you new insights into yourself and your future. Maybe the career ideas you've been considering require graduate or professional degrees.

Graduate study can include everything from a wide range of master's degrees and doctorates to professional degrees in law, medicine, pharmacology, architecture, or social work, among many. These programs differ in terms of the time commitment to completion, the career outcomes, the cost to attend, and so on. Before you plunge into the graduate school pool, it can be helpful to stop and consider all the ramifications. The good news is that you have already done the hard work associated with choosing a graduate program: you have completed the first part of this book where you outlined your strengths, skills, and knowledge as well as the career interests that might have led you to graduate study. So now it's a matter of blending that self-knowledge with what you learn about the graduate school process.

First and foremost, graduate study is career-focused, so start with your career plans. Unlike an undergraduate degree where you have great flexibility in your major, a graduate degree is generally designed to prepare you for a specific career or career field, so you will want to choose wisely.

Many students just assume any graduate degree will help them succeed in the workplace, but that's not always true. What do you want or need to learn? And are there ways to learn without completing a graduate degree? Be careful here. Do your research before you assume that you must have a graduate degree. For instance, many writers assume they must have an MFA before they can write, or students seeking business careers assume they must have an MBA. While both those degrees can help your career, they are not required to enter the job market. Certain business fields and job titles do require an MBA, but there are plenty of ways to start a business career without having one. And you might find that your employer will pay for an MBA—so it could be to your advantage to wait.

When considering graduate or professional schools, always keep your finances in mind. Not only is there a cost to the graduate program (which might add to student loans), but there is also the cost that you are not working a full-time job, you are not receiving the pay and benefits of a job, and you are not moving ahead in your organization. In some cases, you can obtain funding for your degree, which can make it less expensive, but you might need to pay for your own education, which can end up being quite costly.

In addition, it's important that you have a strong understanding of the time needed to complete your degree and the amount of psychological commitment it will require. Pursuing a graduate degree can delay your entry into the workplace, and you can start to feel like you are behind your classmates as they move more directly into their careers. Do you have the resilience needed to tackle the more difficult coursework, including the reading and writing? Are you able to handle criticism—which you are more likely to hear in graduate school—from your professors and your peers. The game is ratcheted up in graduate school, with even greater competition from your peers.

Sample Master's Degrees to Consider

—

Master of Arts (MA) or **Master of Science** (MS) degrees are available in a wide variety of subjects, particularly in liberal arts, social sciences, and humanities fields. An MS degree generally has a strong research component or contains more technical, scientific, or health care–related courses.

In addition, there are many master's degrees that are specific to a profession. Several of these are considered "terminal degrees," meaning you don't need to consider a doctoral degree in the field unless you plan to teach at the college level.

- **Master of Architecture** (MArch) prepares students to qualify for a license as an architect. Courses include such areas as architectural design, history, computer-assisted drafting, and much more.

- **Master of Arts in Liberal Studies** (MA, MALS, MLA/ALM, MLS) is an interdisciplinary degree, often taken by working individuals who want a master's degree but don't want to specialize in a particular career field. This can be a valuable degree for developing new perspectives and insights into your career and life.

- **Master of Business Administration** (MBA) degrees are offered by a wide variety of universities and have lots of specializations and variations. Some focus on new graduates; others are designed for mid-career workers. Specializations include accounting, finance, marketing, and management, among others. It is generally a terminal degree.

- **Master of Education** (MAT, MAEd, MEd, MIT, MSEd) prepares individuals for careers in education. Specializations can include curriculum, instruction, special education, counseling, school psychology, and school administration. Some degrees are short-term (two semesters) and designed for individuals who simply need state certification to teach in a public school system.

- **Master of Engineering** (MEng) provides more in-depth academic or professional training, often combined with internships or research opportunities. Graduates tend to work in industrial fields.

- **Master of Fine Arts** (MFA) is another terminal degree. MFA programs are highly specialized and require careful research. Depending on the institution, they may focus on writing, graphic arts, photography, filmmaking, painting, or other arts. Even then, you will need to do more research. Writing programs, for example, may focus on a few genres such as poetry or literary fiction. One of the appealing elements of MFA degrees is that they provide a certain discipline to creative projects; they have deadlines at the end of each semester. Also, they offer the time needed to work on an artistic project and the opportunity for peer and professional feedback. Strong MFA programs also have good networks and help young professionals connect to their artistic community. By the time the students graduate, they will have portfolios of work to show potential employers or they can embark on their artistic careers. Just do your homework. These programs vary widely in scope and reputation and may not be necessary to pursue your artistic career.

- **Master of Library Science** (MLS, MLIS, MSLS) prepares you for library work in a variety of settings, including private foundations and corporations. If you want to work in a college or university, you might have to complete an additional master's degree in another academic field.

- **Master of Music** (MM/MMus) is a specialty for musicians and can include performance, composition, arranging, and conducting programs.

- **Master of Public Administration** (MPA) is similar to an MBA but with a focus on the public sector. This degree leads to careers in the government, nonprofits, and public or international affairs.

- **Master of Public Health** (MPH) degrees are often interdisciplinary and focus on health-related issues from political, economic, medical, and other perspectives. Specialties might include epidemiology or global health concerns.

- **Master of Social Work** (MSW) is generally considered a terminal degree. Degree holders qualify for professional licenses and specialize in clinical services, agency management, or advocacy/community work.

Building Your Competencies for the Workplace

One way to consider the value of graduate school is to think about the competencies that are needed for the position(s) you're seeking. Review the competencies listed in chapter 3. Will your program help you build them? What specific skills or knowledge do you need in order to succeed in your career field?

In your proposed graduate or professional program, will you:

- Develop the needed competencies for your career?
- Acquire new skills that an employer will appreciate?
- Become familiar with the latest research in your field?
- Work with the latest technology related to your field?
- Learn new software relevant to your field?
- Have the opportunity to work on team projects?
- Practice your presentation skills?
- Have a portfolio of work by the end of your degree?
- Improve your analytic thinking or research skills through this program?

If you're not acquiring or improving key competencies related to your field, the degree might not be what you need.

Alternatives to Traditional Graduate School

One of the things you might discover in answering the questions above is that you don't need to go to graduate school to learn what you want to learn. You might want to seek short-term learning opportunities, such as certificates, to give you the skills you need without the time and expense of graduate study. Are there alternative ways to attend graduate school that might allow you to keep working, building experience, and earning a paycheck?

- Are there online classes (credited or not) that offer the training and knowledge you're seeking?

- Are there seminars or short training courses, or other ways in which you could learn?

- Could you set up your own education with a structured reading program?

- Could you sign up for lessons in art or music? Could you find a local source for writing instruction and inspiration?

- Would it make sense to enroll in just a class or two rather than pursue a full degree program?

- Could you attend school part-time in your home area? Perhaps you're lucky enough to live in a town with a nearby university where you can pursue your degree on a part-time basis. You might want to work at a job and start taking graduate courses one at a time. Many programs are designed for people who are already working and can't get away during the day to take classes. Executive MBA programs are specifically designed, for instance, for busy people who can only take classes on the weekends.

- Do you want to consider online degrees? Just remember that taking online degrees requires a high level of self-control and determination. It's harder to stay motivated when your classes are online and you aren't immersed in the school environment. When you are also working full-time, it can be particularly daunting to get through an online program. If you are considering an online degree, remember that not all degrees are alike. In general, employers prefer online degrees that meet the following criteria:
  - Accredited by a regional accrediting association
  - Come from a brick-and-mortar institution
  - Come from a well-known college with an established brand

Be sure you thoroughly investigate any graduate degree program to make sure your expected outcome is realistic. Do not believe the hype and the advertising or marketing. Get good information by reaching out to alumni from the program.

Making the Decision to Attend Graduate or Professional School

Let's review the typical "good" reasons for pursuing a graduate degree. On the following pages, read through the left column to see which ones fit your reasoning. But then read the right column next to your reasons to clarify your thinking.

"GOOD" REASONS FOR GRADUATE STUDY	BUT ALSO CONSIDER . . .
I have a career plan, and graduate study is part of it.	• How much have you researched and tried out your career plan? • How positive are you that the career field is right for you? • Have you completed an internship or other form of work within the field? • Have you conducted information interviews with individuals currently working in the field? • You may not have enough information to pursue your degree with the confidence needed. Take the time right now to conduct more research.
A graduate degree is essential for my career.	• How do you know? What research have you conducted? • Can you enter your desired career field without the degree? • Certain fields, like the law and medicine, demand a specific degree. But if you're considering a business career, a writing career, or other careers, you might find that you don't need a specific graduate degree.
I have researched the various degree options and know which one will serve my career purpose best.	• Do you need a master's degree or a PhD? • Is a law or medical degree necessary? • What degrees are common in the field you're interested in? • What are the differences between the degrees? • Have you researched the best schools for the degree?
A graduate degree will increase my earning capacity.	• What career field(s) are you interested in? • What are the typical earnings of individuals with the degree you're considering? • What are the salaries related to your intended career field?
A graduate degree will open more opportunities.	• In what way? • What are the typical careers of individuals with this degree? • What career opportunities interest you? • Is this degree a necessary qualification?
A graduate degree will make me more competitive in the job market.	• Are employers requesting a degree you don't have? • Are you lacking certain skills and will this degree provide them? • Are you losing opportunities to people with more degrees? • Do you have evidence that others with this degree are paid better or have a broader spectrum of job titles to choose from?

"GOOD" REASONS FOR GRADUATE STUDY	BUT ALSO CONSIDER . . .
I need to attend the best, or one of the best programs in my field.	• Is having the degree enough or does it need to be from a certain type of school? How prestigious does the school need to be for your career plans? • In some career fields (such as education or government), just having any graduate degree can increase your income. • Your research is important; the "best" school might not have the "best" graduate program for you. Know what differentiates the programs.

Now, let's consider some of the less desirable reasons for going to graduate school and why you should reconsider if they are yours. Be honest with yourself: are these some of the reasons you're planning to go to graduate school? If they are, take the time to explore your motives more carefully. Can you focus on the previous reasons and do your research? There's nothing necessarily wrong with following family legacies or adding to your resume, but make sure you are being true to yourself in this process.

LESS DESIRABLE REASONS	WHY YOU SHOULD THINK THIS THROUGH:
It's what my family wants. Everyone thinks I should get a_____ degree.	They may be right. But they're not the ones who have to do the work or pay the tuition. Do you want to pursue this degree? And does the degree lead to a career you want to pursue? How much pressure are you under? Consider getting the support of a counselor if family expectations are having an impact on your general happiness.
I don't know what career I want, so I'd like to keep studying more.	This is a common reaction to the fear of making career decisions. You are comfortable with studying and school, so what's a few more years? This is a rather passive approach to career development and focuses more on what you're avoiding rather than what you're moving toward.
I really hate the job search. I think it will be easier if I have a master's degree.	This is similar to the previous reason. Because the job search is an unknown and anxiety-provoking, it seems easier to just stay in school. You tell yourself it will help your job search, but you don't really know this.

continued →

LESS DESIRABLE REASONS	WHY YOU SHOULD THINK THIS THROUGH:
I want to become a college professor so I must have a PhD.	First, research the academic career path. In what field do you plan to study and ultimately teach? How many job openings are there each year? If you plan a career as a professor, you need to speak with your professors and get their advice on everything from the pros/cons of the field to what schools to attend. Higher education is evolving rapidly, and the role of the professor is changing as well. It is harder to find traditional tenure-track positions in almost every field. Many recent graduates have had to enter adjunct careers, which do not pay as well and don't offer the job security of tenure-track positions.
It has always been my passion to study ____.	Passion is great. Passion gives energy. Passion provides motivation. But passion isn't always the best career guide. You will still need to get a job when you graduate, so make sure you have a reasonable career plan to follow while you pursue your passion. If your talents are in the artistic realm, get an objective evaluation of your work. You want to honor your career dreams, but you don't want to build up more debt if you won't be able to find work after you're done.
There are so many programs out there; they must really be necessary.	Advertising for graduate programs is everywhere and can make you think you must have one of these degrees. But don't mistake the number of programs for either quality or necessity. Do your homework.
My friends are all going to grad school. I should, too.	Again, this is your search, not your friends'. It's tempting to follow the herd, so to speak, but be sure it's for your reasons and not because everyone is doing it. Going to law school because your friends are all applying isn't the best way to begin a legal career.
My school keeps advertising these one-year master's programs. I'd like to stay at my school for another year after graduation.	Many schools have found that short one-year master's degrees are appealing to students and, quite frankly, a good income resource for the school. Sometimes they are based on learning a specific skill, like coding, data analytics, or building general skills in management. The questions to ask yourself are: Do I need this degree? Do I need the skills I will learn in this program? Will it help me enter the profession I seek? Is it worth the time and the money? Does the program have good connections to employers? If possible, talk to graduates of the program and ask if they would do it again. Ask them how valuable the program was for their career.

Creating a SWOT Analysis Thought Organizer for Graduate Study

A SWOT analysis is a great way to start thinking about graduate study. The SWOT divides your thinking into four categories: Your Strengths, Weaknesses, Opportunities, and Threats. By using this logical Thought Organizer, you can quickly create an assessment of what you need to do before applying to graduate school.

• • •

Brianna is a junior English major interested in a career related to mental health. She knows that most careers related to that field require advanced degrees, and she also knows she has several options. She has already taken a sample GRE test and thinks she will do well on the real exam. So she starts by creating a SWOT to highlight the areas she could develop over the next few years to make her application to graduate school stronger. Here's what she created:

SWOT Diagram

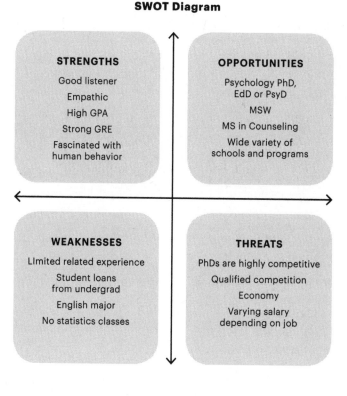

STRENGTHS
Good listener
Empathic
High GPA
Strong GRE
Fascinated with
human behavior

OPPORTUNITIES
Psychology PhD,
EdD or PsyD
MSW
MS in Counseling
Wide variety of
schools and programs

WEAKNESSES
LImited related experience
Student loans
from undergrad
English major
No statistics classes

THREATS
PhDs are highly competitive
Qualified competition
Economy
Varying salary
depending on job

As Brianna examines her SWOT profile, she realizes she needs to consider several actions over her final semesters in college:

- *She has student loans, and the salary she might receive in the field of mental health services will vary widely depending on the degree she receives and the job she pursues. She will need to keep this in mind when choosing her career, particularly given that graduate school might add to her debt load.*

- *She will likely need to build up her experience related to mental health or clinical research. She might consider volunteering at a nearby hospital, nonprofit agency, or clinic, or participating in research projects at her college.*

- *She plans to investigate the psychology and statistics courses she could take to build up her knowledge. She could also look at related courses, like neuroscience or cognitive science. Taking these courses will help her confirm and refine her interests.*

- *She needs to examine her English major further to see if it might actually be an asset to her application. After all, what better way to learn about the human condition than through memoirs and the interesting characters found in literature?*

- *She needs to research the various degree options to determine which ones have the courses that interest her and lead to careers she prefers. She needs to review any prerequisites or required majors to enter the different programs.*

- *She will also double-check the salaries in those fields and the overall job outlook.*

- *She needs to speak with alumni from her college who are working in the different fields of interests: social workers, counselors, and psychologists. She can see if they have shadowing or internship opportunities as well, suggestions for graduate programs, or other advice that will be helpful.*

• • •

Now that Brianna has a better idea of her overall situation, she can develop a plan for the next few semesters to continue exploring her career and graduate school interests. By her senior year, she should have a much stronger application profile, and a clearer idea of the career that most interests her.

Getting Ready for Graduate School: Investigate Your Options

If you determine that graduate or professional study is in the cards for you, then you will want to do even more research into the specific degree you are seeking.

1 **Talk to your professors.** If you're planning to study the same subject as your undergraduate major, your professors can often provide the best guidance for graduate study.

2 **Visit your career center.** Many career centers offer guidance on graduate school as part of their overall career planning mission.

3 **Identify the key schools and degrees that best fit your career goals.** Are you seeking programs that are research-based or more practice-based? Are you planning an academic (teaching) career or a practitioner career? What are the career outcomes of the graduates of this program?

4 **Investigate any scholarships or financial support available.** Does the school offer graduate assistanceships or teaching assistanceships? Is low-cost housing available?

5 **Identify the research conducted at the institutions you're considering.** Go to the specific degree program you're seeking and look at the profiles of the professors in the department. Many will either list their current research and publications, or they will attach a vita (resume) to their webpage and you can see their focus. How closely is their research aligned with what you are interested in studying, publishing, or practicing?

6 **Investigate the quality of the graduate program.** How selective are the programs you're considering? Keep in mind that excellent graduate degree programs might be found in a variety of universities, regardless of the university's overall ranking. The best master's degree in your field might be at a state university, for instance, rather than an elite private school.

7 **Check out the various graduate school guides, including *US News & World Report*.** They can provide overall helpful information and point out programs and universities you might not have considered. Don't rely on their information exclusively, however. Always check

with alumni from the program, your professors, and others who will have first-hand knowledge.

8 **Thoroughly read the website for the programs you're considering.** Review the length of the program, how many classes you'll need to take, and what the content of those classes will be. As you read through this material, pay attention to your energy level. Are you getting excited about the opportunity to learn the subject matter, or are you starting to feel bored or losing energy as you read the course descriptions. Does it sound like you would thrive in this program, or do you suspect you might be wasting your time? It is so important to pay attention to your energy and thoughts as you go through the graduate school material. If it's not exciting you about the potential opportunities, it might be smart to wait a while or seek a different program.

How to Apply to Graduate School

1 **Work with your career center or other pre-professional office** (pre-law, pre-med, and so on) relevant to your area of interest. Don't try to do it alone.

2 **Select the most appropriate programs for your career and/or research interests.** Note their requirements:

- Do you have the grade point average (GPA) necessary for entry?
- If you have taken admissions tests, are your scores in line with what they accept?
- Do they require you to have work experience? And do you have the preferred experience?
- Have you taken the necessary courses for admission?

3 **Check your latest grade point average.** You can look into your GPA at your registrar's office and note how it compares with the graduate school's admission profile. If your GPA is significantly lower than the average, you will likely find it difficult to be admitted. But if your GPA is only slightly below their mean, you might find that other factors, like strong essays or experience, will enhance your application. (This is another reason to consider working for a year or two before graduate school. Not only will you acquire experience and additional letters of reference, but the longer you are away from school, the less important your grades will be.)

4 Read everything about the application process for each school.
In some cases you'll be able to fill out a standard application for
many schools, but in others you will need to apply to each program
individually. Many have rolling admissions, but keep in mind that
assistanceships and other types of scholarships or financial support
can go early, so don't wait until the final deadline.

5 Determine if you need to take any admissions exams. Decide if
you need to take a prep course to prepare for them. Are you a self-
starter who can independently schedule yourself to study, or would
you benefit from a more structured program? Once you get your
scores, you will have a better idea of the program(s) that will likely
admit you.

6 Research the financing available. This will differ at each institution.
Look for teaching or research assistanceships, grants, or other funding that might be available.

7 Line up your letters of recommendation. If you haven't already
done this, speak to your professors about writing letters of recommendation. Professors take time to write these letters carefully, and
it's inappropriate to ask them to write under a tight deadline.

**8 Complete the application, including any essays, in a timely
manner.** Try not to wait until the deadline to apply.

Writing Your Application and Essay for Graduate or Professional Schools

Each program has its own application essay requirement. The essays
requested will vary in length and may be unstructured or focused on a
response to certain questions. **Always follow the directions exactly. If
they indicate a word limit, don't go beyond it. If a specific question
is asked, answer it.** Your essay is a chance to demonstrate your personality, history, interests, writing skills, and career plans.

As you write your essay, here are some ideas to consider:

1 Check on the resources available at your school to help with
graduate school essays. Many schools have writing centers or even
pre-med or pre-law career offices that can help you. Your career
center likely works with graduate school essays, too.

2   Start with the exercises you completed earlier in this book. Refer to the stories you wrote in chapter 3. Are any of the situations you wrote about useful for including in your essay? Also, refer to your Backpack Inventory list. What items do you want to be sure to include in your essay?

3   Plan to write a unique essay for each graduate program, if possible. Make sure you tailor your responses to fit the program and the unique features of their degree.

4   Think beyond the graduate school experience. What is the likely career field you will enter? What are the characteristics of people in that career field? How will this program prepare you for that field? What specific elements of the program are important and significant for you? You can include some of your ideas in your essay. Just keep in mind that, depending on your program, it is appropriate to stay open to other career opportunities. You can indicate that your current career plan is _____, but you are hoping to gain new knowledge that might change your career direction.

5   After reviewing the essay question you're answering (or the open essay requirement), make a list of key points you want to cover. Use the list below if needed.

- Try not to repeat what is already in your resume or other documents.

- Think about the personality traits or skills you have that you want them to know. How does your essay reveal these traits without necessarily directly identifying them? For instance, indicating the work you've done with data analytics or creating apps automatically demonstrates your tech and quantitative skills.

- Link up the skills and traits listed in the chart on the opposite page with stories or examples that illustrate them. Which ones describe you—and why would your graduate program care that you have those traits? You must make a connection between your skills and traits to the program you're seeking.

Achievement-oriented	Committed	Communicator
Compassionate	Creative	Critical thinker
Empathic	Ethical	Flexible
Focused	Genuine	Hardworking
Innovative	Insightful	Leadership skills
Logical	Mature	Organized
Passionate	Positive thinker	Quantitative skills
Quick learner	Research skills	Responsible
Team player	Tech skills	Writing skills

6   Think about your essay as telling a compelling and convincing story. How can you hook the reader with an interesting opening sentence or paragraph? What is the overall theme or message you want to convey? What is your point? What is unique about you and your experiences?

7   Use the essay as an opportunity to give an admissions committee the chance to see a new side of you. Share information about volunteer experiences, for example, if they are relevant to your degree.

8   Proofread. Proofread. Proofread. Ask others to read your essay. Try reading it out loud to see how it flows. If you stumble over your words when reading it, you probably need to rewrite that sentence.

Managing Your Career While in Grad School

So you made it into graduate or professional school—congratulations! But this doesn't mean your job search ends. Not even temporarily. As much as you are enjoying your graduate study, the classes you are taking, and the knowledge you are building, it's important to keep your end goal in mind. You want to graduate and you want to find a job in the career field you have been studying. But having the degree isn't always enough. Don't allow your time in school to be an escape from your career planning. The more you keep you career in mind as you pursue your degree, the more likely you will have a better career outcome. Here are some basic tips to keep in mind as you go through your graduate program.

Timeline for Graduate School

The chart below presents an ideal plan for considering and applying to graduate school. But it's not the only plan. Many students don't decide on graduate school until their junior or senior year. And many graduate schools would prefer that you acquire some real-world experience before applying. But if you know you want to go to graduate school, this timeline can help you plan the process. Just know that if you decide at the beginning of your senior year, for example, you'll just have to work through the list for the previous years and catch up as best as you can.

First/ Sophomore Year	• Take classes of interest, focus on career ideas • Acquire experience • Information interview to build kowledge • Ask professors about graduate school • Attend programs offered by career center or your department/major • Try to achieve the best GPA you can—the higher your GPA, the more schools you will qualify for
Junior Year	• Start researching potential degrees and programs • Check out their admissions requirements • Start preparing for any entrance exams • Note required dates for applications • Check out financial aid, including assistanceships or scholarships • Talk to professors about graduate study
Summer between Junior/ Senior Years	• Prepare for entrance exams and consider taking if possible • Find a job, internship, or experience related to career interests • Consider visiting schools of interest and meeting with faculty or admissions representatives
Senior Year	• Create a calendar with deadlines for specific programs • Determine what you need to do before applying; retake exams if needed • Create a list of schools you plan to apply to • Determine which schools fit your test score/grades • Write your essays • Contact faculty, administrators, or supervisors for letters of recommendation

- **Take the classes most relevant to your future plans.** You will likely have a chance to take some elective courses, so choose them carefully. If needed, investigate whether you can take classes offered outside your major or department. Find classes that will teach you valuable skills or competencies needed in the job market.

- **Acquire relevant experience.** Keeping your future career plans in mind, what experiences outside the classroom would build your resume?

    - If you plan a teaching career, for example, are you currently teaching? Keep track of your teaching evaluations and keep a journal of interesting students, stories, or situations you've encountered. They will be great sources of stories for future interviews.

    - If you're planning a research-based career, are you part of significant research projects? Are you conducting your own research? What can you do to improve your research skills, data analytic or statistical abilities, or other skills.

- **Network and connect.** Use your time in graduate school to develop connections with your professors (who often hear about job opportunities), alumni from your program (who might be able to hire you or offer an internship), and professionals in the field who visit your school to give a talk. Use LinkedIn and other social media platforms to build your reputation as well as your outreach to professionals in your field. Join the professional organization(s) related to your career. Attend their conferences or take advantage of any career guidance they might provide.

- **Publish and present.** Graduate school is an excellent time to develop your writing and speaking skills. Seek out opportunities to be part of a research study where your name can be added to the author's list. Write articles for social media sites or your own webpage to demonstrate your knowledge of your field or career. Seek opportunities to present at conferences related to your field.

- **Develop a go-to-market strategy.** More than ever, it's important to use this Parachute System to develop your plan for entering the job market. Keep this plan in mind throughout your time in graduate school. Don't wait until the semester before you graduate to start thinking about how you'll handle your job search. By following the Parachute System, you may not even need to do a job search: you might have an employer seek you out!

The Job Search After Grad School

The job search after graduate school can follow the exact trajectory described in this book, so the Parachute System will work well for you. But if you're having trouble, consider the following ideas.

- Don't assume the degree will get you the job. You still need to show that you have the skills, knowledge, and expertise the employer is seeking. In some cases, you may find the degree doesn't help you; employers might be afraid you'll want higher pay or that you might get bored. This shouldn't be an issue if you have followed the Parachute System and know your skills and are applying for the right position. But if there's a disconnect between what you studied and what you are seeking, you will need to explain your reasoning to an employer. Use your Backpack Inventory to focus on your skills and knowledge.

- The job market may not be as rosy as you hoped. For instance, if you're finishing a doctorate and hoping to teach at a college or university, you might find a disappointing lack of positions. And the competition may be fierce. This is where your Parachute planning can be helpful. You can start to look for alternate careers that might be just as interesting as teaching would have been.

- A graduate degree can place an additional psychological burden on you. You might feel even more pressure to find the "perfect" job, now that you have spent even more time in school. If the jobs you're seeking aren't readily available, you might experience regrets, a lack of confidence, disappointments, or even some shame or guilt about your reasons for going to graduate school. Just know that these feelings will pass. You can use the Parachute System to find a great opportunity, and your graduate study will not have been in vain. Focus on your acquired strengths and skills to give yourself a motivational boost when needed.

- Broaden your career ideas if your chosen field isn't open. You might have entered your graduate program with one career in mind, but you don't have to stay with that idea. Notice what your classmates are doing and what other graduates of your program have done. Perhaps it's time to look at alternative careers. How could your talents be applied to a variety of settings? Consider opportunities in education, business, the nonprofit sector, government, technology, communications, and literary or entrepreneurial settings.

If you have followed the Parachute System, your transition into and out of graduate school and into the workplace can be seamless— you know, like falling slowly and safely to the ground with your parachute.

CHAPTER 12

Land a Gap Experience

Gap experiences are popular with students who need a break from whatever they have been doing and are looking for a way to experience something new—a foreign location, a short-term volunteer or work experience, a chance to fulfill a purpose or mission, or a chance to fulfill a creative passion or dream. Designed to be relatively short in length, as in the "gap" between your senior year and first professional work experience, gap experiences often represent a pause in one's ordinary life, and can provide an opportunity for self-development, personal growth, and learning. Gap experiences can be done any time, but usually happen during the year between high school and college, or between college and graduate school, or between college and full-time professional employment. In some cases, you can defer your admission to graduate school for one year while you pursue your gap experience.

Gap experiences can take place anywhere from a cruise ship to a foreign country to your home community. A gap experience can provide cultural immersion through volunteer programs where your work can have a direct impact on someone's life. This could include service-learning opportunities working with the homeless, tutoring, or teaching in inner-city or rural schools. Popular programs such as Teach for America provide an opportunity to teach children, even if teaching isn't your ultimate career goal. Gap experiences are only limited by your imagination. Sometimes gap experiences are temporary jobs, like being an au pair (nanny) or teaching English as a second language abroad. You can go through organized programs, or just develop your own. Even a job can serve as a gap experience between college and graduate/professional school.

How would you like to take a gap year and:

- Work at a summer camp helping children who have cancer
- Be an au pair in China
- Teach snowboarding in New Zealand
- Be a tour guide on a railroad in Alaska
- Volunteer in a wildlife conservation program in Africa
- Be a Fulbright Scholar in India
- Study abroad in Italy
- Work at a pub in England
- Take a post-graduate program at a university to prepare for medical school
- Volunteer to teach kindergarten in Bali

All of these experiences and more are possible during a gap year.

Gap experiences can give you the mental and physical space needed to detach from your current life. By doing this, you may clarify your plans for the future, including graduate school plans. You might learn you aren't as interested in graduate school when you return. You might find a new career plan. Or you might find that the plans you developed previously are perfect, and you're returning to school or work with renewed energy and enthusiasm. A gap experience, if funded, can even provide additional money for graduate study. Depending on your experience, a gap year can even improve your employment opportunities. Your gap experience can be the source of an interesting addition to your resume and social media profile and can provide potentially interesting interview stories.

Despite the emphasis on taking a break, gap experiences are not meant to be spent on your sofa watching *Law & Order SVU* reruns. That's not a gap year; that's just hiding out. A gap year is also not just a vacation. While there can be an element of rest, relaxation, and, of course, adventure, a gap year is ultimately meant to help you refresh and rethink.

Remember back in chapter 2 when you analyzed your interests and considered your values—what did you decide was really important to you? Refer to the diagram on page 51 again to refresh your memory.

If you already filled in that diagram with your values, revisit it and see if what you chose still fits your current thinking. If not, read it and determine which areas are most important to you. Would you like to do a gap experience that would immerse you in that interest, cause, or purpose?

A gap year can give you the chance to explore those interests and values in depth. You can volunteer, travel to another country, explore and help the environment, or explore your creativity and complete an artistic, musical, or writing project. Are some of your interests or values not really job-related? Maybe you put down a value of spirituality or a religion-related cause, but you don't plan to work in that field. Would taking a gap year give you the opportunity to explore that interest or value?

Usually the main challenge of doing a gap year is the cost. If you're not earning money, the experience can be quite expensive, particularly if you're traveling a lot or attempting to live abroad. You will find options for many structured programs at the end of this chapter, and many of them are "pay to play" so to speak. You have to pay a fee in order to participate in the experience. The good news is that once you pay that fee, a lot of your other expenses (like housing and food) are paid for, so ultimately you might spend less money than you otherwise would. But any time you are paying a fee, make sure you have investigated the organization thoroughly. Search it on the internet for any warnings or ratings. Don't always trust the ratings on the site; see if you can find independent verification. You can check the Better Business Bureau if the organization is based in the US.

Another concern you might have is how you will explain your experience to a potential employer or graduate school. Fortunately, that is under your control. No matter what your gap experience is, you will learn so much about yourself and whatever project you're involved in, that you can tell the stories about your experience in a way that will appeal to an employer or graduate school. Just be prepared to discuss the skills you acquired and the renewed commitment to your work.

Developing Your Gap Experience

To start thinking about designing your gap experience, consider your purpose. Why are you interested in completing a gap experience? What motivates you?

Here are some questions to consider.

- What's the purpose? Expanding your resume? Experiencing a new country or culture? Living independently? Learning a new skill? Focusing on a beloved hobby such as music, art, or writing?
- Why does this interest you?
- What will motivate you to do the necessary research and follow through on your plans?
- Is your gap year plan personal or professional? If professional, how does your gap year plan fit into your future plans?

Once you have an idea of the type of gap experience you'd like to pursue, it's time to plan it.

- Talk to your family about your ideas. You don't necessarily need their permission, but it would be helpful to have their support. Particularly if you are planning to travel abroad, can your family help if there's an emergency and you have to fly home unexpectedly?
- Start by defining the time period.
- Are you interested in a structured program, or would you rather do your experience independently?
- Are you going alone or with others?
- Will you be earning any money during the time or will you need to rely on your own savings or funds from your family or other sources?
- What will your gap experience cost? Consider any travel funds, the general cost of living wherever you are, and any other expenses you might incur.

Want to brainstorm your ideas for your gap experience? Try creating a mind map Thought Organizer (see diagram, page 250). Start with your general idea in the center and then put various ideas into circles and draw lines connecting your ideas. Take a look at Benjamin's story and the mind map he created.

• • •

Benjamin is a senior engineering science major, and he doesn't know what he wants to study or what career he might pursue. His major prepared him for a variety of careers in business or government, including city planning or consulting. It's December, and he'd like to have something lined up when he graduates in May. When he completed the Values Exercise in chapter 2, what stood out was his love of animals, particularly horses, and his interest in doing something to preserve the environment. His engineering science degree could definitively come in handy in a conservation or sustainability position. He decides he needs a year to do something completely different from studying engineering, so he's thinking about taking a gap year. He created a mind map to develop his ideas. He started by listing what was most important to do during his gap year: travel somewhere new, earn money, work in the outdoors, and somehow be around horses. Once he had that basic frame, he started brainstorming ideas that fit those categories.

Mind Map Thought Organizer

Benjamin had always gone to the beach in the summers with his family; now he wanted to try the mountains. He thought about every place where there might be horses and started listing those. Then he thought about how he could earn money, and the idea popped into his head of working at a dude ranch or a state park where people go on trail rides. From there he hit the internet and found a variety of options. Using a site called CoolWorks (https://www.coolworks.com), he found jobs in the Pacific Northwest, Canada, and Colorado ranging from horse wrangler to horseback guide to leading a horseback-riding instruction program for a Girl Scout camp. The good news is that not only will he be paid for these experiences, many of the sites offer free housing so he might be able to save money for graduate school. All the jobs start in the summer, so he's applying over his holiday break between semesters and hopes to have *his gap plans all set up by mid-spring. Once he starts his gap experience, Benjamin is going to check out what sustainability and conservation activities are going on in the area, and he will volunteer to work with them.*

MY GAP EXPERIENCE

So now it's time to design *your* gap experience. Take a few minutes to answer the following questions. Re-create this form on your computer or in your notebook. It's okay not to know anything for sure; just jot down the various ideas you have at the moment.

What is my goal for my gap year? What would I like to say I did by the end of my experience?

_____

_____

How could I accomplish this goal?

_____

_____

Where would I travel or live? (List the cities or countries)

_____

_____

Is my experience structured or independent?

_____

_____

If structured, what organizations or groups will I connect with?

_____

_____

If independent, what does my experience look like?

_____

_____

Now that you've completed this form and have some basic ideas, if you haven't done this already, try making your own mind map to further explore all your ideas and see what connections you might be able to make. Start with a blank piece of paper and place your major concepts (refer to Benjamin's map for ideas) and then fill in your thoughts as they develop. See how many of your ideas can be connected into an overall pattern or concept for your gap year.

Researching Gap Opportunities

One of the best ways to start your research about a gap year is to go online to the many sites devoted to the gap experience. As you read through the various descriptions and opportunities, take note of your energy and interests. Which ones sound like a great adventure or experience? Which ones sound like they would take you out of your normal comfort zone and present you with new opportunities to learn? Be careful about gap experiences that seem like something you "should" do. A gap experience is not about "should." It's about getting away from those "shoulds" and finding something that will energize you and fill your soul. Only you can determine what that might be.

One of the best websites for college students considering a gap experience is from the Yale University's Office of Career Strategy (https://ocs.yale.edu/channels/gap-year-short-term-opportunities). The site has an extensive listing of agencies, fellowships, and other opportunities to consider. In the box on the opposite page, you'll find a wide variety of opportunities to check out. As you read them, keep your energy and motivation in mind. Which sites offer opportunities that would make an amazing gap year for you?

A gap year can provide an excellent opportunity to refresh and regroup, clarify your career and graduate study plans, and provide an unforgettable once-in-a-lifetime experience.

Sites for Potential Gap Year Opportunities

These sites offer gap-related information, ideas, and services, and many offer a multitude of opportunities around the world. Some connect you to part-time or full-time jobs. Some are the "pay to play" types of experiences. Use this list to research the opportunities and see which ones appeal to you. Notice your energy: are you getting excited reading about a particular experience? Take that as a clue and look for related opportunities. Always investigate an experience thoroughly before committing any funds.

Achievement First	https://www.achievementfirst.org
African Impact	https://www.africanimpact.com
America India Foundation Fellowship	https://aif.org/fellowship
American Jewish Committee	https://www.ajc.org/careers
Americorps	https://www.nationalservice.gov/programs/americorps
Blue Ventures	https://blueventures.org
Bunac	https://www.bunac.org/usa
Carpe Diem Education	https://www.carpediemeducation.org
Chegg Internships	https://www.internships.com
City Year	https://www.cityyear.org
Conservation Travel Africa	https://conservationtravelafrica.org
CoolWorks	https://www.coolworks.com
Cross Cultural Solutions	https://www.crossculturalsolutions.org
Disney World Internship Program	https://jobs.disneycareers.com/professional-internships
EnRoute Consulting	http://enroutegapyear.com

continued →

Frontier	https://frontiergap.com
Gapforce	https://gapforce.org/us
Gapwork	http://gapwork.com
Gapyear	https://www.gapyear.com
Go overseas	https://www.gooverseas.com
GoAbroad	https://www.goabroad.com
Impact Trip	https://impactrip.com
International Volunteer HQ	https://www.volunteerhq.org
National Tour Association	https://ntaonline.com
Outward Bound	https://www.outwardbound.org
Pacific Discovery	https://www.pacificdiscovery.org
Peace Corps	https://www.peacecorps.gov
ProFellow	https://www.profellow.com
Projects Abroad	https://www.projects-abroad.org
Project Trust	https://projecttrust.org.uk
Raleigh International	https://raleighinternational.org
Real Gap Experience	https://www.realgap.co.uk
RSVP Caribbean Volunteers	https://www.rsvpcaribbean.com
Service Year Alliance	https://serviceyear.org
Teaching English as a Foreign Language	https://www.tefl.com
United Planet	https://www.unitedplanet.org
UN volunteers	https://www.unv.org
USA Gap Year Fairs	https://www.gooverseas.com/gap-year/usa-fairs
Washington Center for Internships	https://twc.edu
Youth International	https://www.youthinternational.org

Conclusion

Final Instructions for the Trip

———

You made it! Congratulations on finishing this book.

If you simply read the book, you've learned a lot about the search. I hope you feel more confident and ready to tackle the job market, no matter what it looks like. But to get the most out of this book, consider going back to the beginning and completing the exercises. You will be surprised at how much more you will learn about yourself and where you fit in the workplace.

The best part of learning the Parachute System is that you can use it for the rest of your life. Every time you think about changing a job, changing your career, going to graduate school, or any other future ideas, this system will be here to help you. You will always start a search with *you* first. Each time you revisit the system, you will be new with additional skills, knowledge, and interests.

Remember this system is designed to work regardless of the job market. You just have to double down and work harder when the job market is tight.

By focusing on your skills and knowledge, you will continue to find success in the workplace; and if you keep in touch with your interests and values, you will also find happiness.

You are never alone in this search. People will help you every step of the way if you simply ask. And let this book be your companion as well.

Safe landings!

Notes

1 Neff, Kristin. "The Motivational Power of Self-Compassion" Self-Compassion.org. 15 August 2019. https://self-compassion.org/the-motivational-power-of-self-compassion.

2 Hess, Abigail J. "The 6 Most Popular College Majors." CNBC, CNBC, 15 Dec. 2017, www.cnbc.com/2017/12/15/the-6-most-popular-college-majors.html.

3 "Most Meaningful Majors." PayScale, 2019, www.payscale.com/college-salary-report/most-meaningful-majors?orderBy=percentHighMeaning&%3Bamp%3Bascending=false.

4 Abel, Jason R., and Richard Deitz. "Agglomeration and Job Matching among College Graduates." Federal Reserve Bank of New York Staff Reports, No. 587, Federal Reserve Bank of New York, Dec. 2012, Revised Dec. 2014, www.newyorkfed.org/medialibrary/media/research/staff_reports/sr587.pdf.

5 NACE. "Are College Graduates 'Career Ready'?" National Association of Colleges and Employers, 19 Feb. 2018, www.naceweb.org/career-readiness/competencies/are-college-graduates-career-ready.

6 Friedman, Zack. "50% Of Millennials Are Moving Back Home With Their Parents After College." Forbes, 6 June 2019, www.forbes.com/sites/zackfriedman/2019/06/06/millennials-move-back-home-college/#51612ee1638a.

7 Jaschik, Scott. "Well-Prepared in Their Own Eyes." *Inside Higher Ed*, 20 Jan. 2015, www.insidehighered.com/news/2015/01/20/study-finds-big-gaps-between-student-and-employer-perceptions.

Acknowledgments

Thank you to my agent, Bonnie Solow, who never fails to guide me brilliantly through the publishing process. And to my excellent editors Ashley Pierce and copyeditor Andrea Chesman who made the writing and editing process go smoothly in spite of the world events of 2020.

Thank you to my students and colleagues at the excellent schools where I have had the honor of directing their career centers: Vanderbilt University, Wake Forest University, The University of Texas at Austin, and Dickinson College. I cherish the many relationships and friendships that I developed throughout my time at each school.

Finally, I want to thank the National Association of Colleges and Employers (NACE) for their pivotal role in furthering the careers of so many college and university professionals. The people at NACE have provided me with support, guidance, education, and fellowship throughout my career and I am eternally grateful.

About the Author

Katharine Brooks, EdD, is an award-winning, nationally certified counselor and career coach who is currently the Evans Family Executive Director of the Career Center for Vanderbilt University. She has also directed career centers at The University of Texas at Austin, Wake Forest University, and Dickinson College. She is the author of *You Majored in What? Designing Your Path From College to Career* and co-author of *What Color Is Your Parachute? 2021*. She writes a blog, Career Transitions, for *Psychology Today*.

Index

A
action verbs, 135–36
anxiety, 126

B
Backpack
  contents of, 39
  as first part of Parachute System, 3
  generating career ideas with,
    104–5
  importance of full, 97, 192
  packing, 97
benefits, 92, 208, 209
big rocks, 16–17
business, starting your own, 128
business school. *See* graduate or
  professional school

C
Campus Activities Exercise, 42–46
career centers, 10, 14, 131, 207, 216
career development
  graduate school and, 241, 243
  unending nature of, 6
Career Interest Analyzer, 41–42
career readiness, 57–60
careers
  combining, 107–8
  generating ideas about, 104–8
  hidden opportunities for, 109–10
  jobs vs., 3
  majors and, 24
  meta-industry categories for,
    111–23
challenges
  Challenges Thought Organizer, 13
  common, 11–12

Coping with Challenges Thought
  Organizer, 20
  overcoming, 13–19
  personal, 12
choices
  evaluating, 123
  lack of, 125
  landing spot metaphor for, 100–101
  learning and, 101–3
  planning diagram for, 126–27
  psychological traps and, 125–26
classes
  choosing, 32–33
  prerequisite, 21
  skills and competencies from,
    66–69
  weed-out, 37
commute times, 197
comparisons, avoiding, 11
competencies
  building, 69, 230
  career readiness and, 57–60
  from classes, 66–69
  identifying, 66–67
  list of, 58
  on resumes, 136
consulting career interviews, 188, 189
conversations
  anxiety and, 163
  importance of, 161–62
  practicing, 163–65
  types of, 162
  See also information interviews;
    job interviews; networking;
    pitches
Coping with Challenges Thought
  Organizer, 20
cover letters, 156–60

online, 217–18
personal goals and, 213–14
interviews. *See* information
interviews; job interviews

J

job interviews
appearance and, 174–76
for consulting careers, 188, 189
from employers' point of view, 174
for financial careers, 188–89
following up after, 210
information interviews vs., 168
interpersonal skills and, 176–77
on-campus recruiting and,
199–202
by phone, 179
practicing, 180, 186
preparing for, 177, 178, 180, 186
questions during, 177–78
resumes and, 176
stories for, 183–85
tips for, 178, 180–81, 183–84,
186–87
virtual, 182
job offers
lack of, 210
managing, 207–9
verbal vs. in writing, 208
jobs
careers vs., 3
dream, 104, 192
on-campus, 65
summer, 211, 219–23
job search
challenges of, 5, 11–12
for college students vs. others, 4
as community experience, 144
concerns about, 1–3
from employers' point of view, 124
after graduate school, 244–45

importance of interests and
values for, 38
individualizing, 19–20
as Neanderthal process, 3
other activities and, 18
philosophy for, 7
Preparation Form, 194–96
start of, 38
traditional approach to, 199–202
See also Parachute System

K

keywords
in resumes, 135
in social media, 146–47, 154
knowledge
building, with short-term
experiences, 213
identifying areas of, 70–72
importance of, 56
skills vs., 55

L

law school. *See* graduate or
professional school
leadership experience, 140–41
life purpose, 50–53
LinkedIn
creating account for, 152
guidelines for, 151
ideas for using, 153–54
improving profile for, 155–56
information interviews and, 172
popularity of, 146, 148
resumes vs., 130

M

majors
career choice and, 24
changing, 24
combining, 31

self-compassion, 14–15
Seven Stories Exercise, 60–64
short-term experiences
  benefits of, 128
  finding, 214–18
  personal goals and, 213–14
  types of, 211
  See also gap experiences;
    internships; summer
    experiences
skills
  building, 69, 213
  from classes, 66–69
  identifying, 61–64, 66–67
  importance of, 56
  knowledge vs., 55
  in LinkedIn profile, 156
  making full use of, 56
  Parachute Skills Grid, 61–64
  in resumes, 138
  talent vs., 56
  types of, 56–57
social media
  guidelines for, 149–51
  importance of, 145–46
  information interviews and, 172
  keywords in, 146–47
  planning, 148
  See also individual social media
STAR technique, 183–84
stories
  for interviews, 183–85
  Seven Stories Exercise, 60–64
strengths, knowing, 181, 183
stress, managing, 17–18
summer experiences, 211, 219–23
SWOT analysis, 235–36

T
talent, 56
to-do's, 16–17
Twenty Things I Like Exercise, 40
Twitter, 148, 151

V
values
  exploring online, 47
  identifying, 46–50, 93
  importance of, for job search,
    38, 46
  life purpose and, 50–53
virtual interviews, 182

W
weed-out classes, 37
work settings, preferred, 73–74,
  79–83

Y
The Yet Thought Organizer, 19
YouTube, 148, 151

THE COMPLETE PARACHUTE LIBRARY

A quick guide to the job search, for when time is of the essence.

A slender guide to writing a winning resume and cover letter that will help you land interviews.

A slender guide to help you ace the interview and land your dream job.

A guide to help students zero in on the perfect major or career.

The world's most popular and bestselling career guide.

Practical tools and exercises for a prosperous retirement.

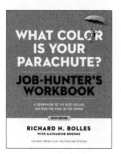

A fill-in edition of the famous Flower Exercise.

Learn to use the internet effectively for all aspects of your job-hunt.

A complete guide for practicing or aspiring career counselors.

Visit parachutebook.com and JobHuntersBible.com

Available from Ten Speed Press wherever books are sold.
www.tenspeed.com

To Chip—Who is always there

Published in the United States by Ten Speed Press, an imprint of
Random House, a division of Penguin Random House LLC, New York.
www.tenspeed.com

Ten Speed Press and the Ten Speed Press colophon are registered
trademarks of Penguin Random House LLC.

Library of Congress Cataloging-in-Publication Data
    Names: Brooks, Katharine, author.
    Title: What color is your parachute? for college : pave your path
    from major to meaningful work / Katharine Brooks.
    Description: First edition. | California : Ten Speed Press, [2021]
    Identifiers: LCCN 2020042838 | ISBN 9781984857569 (trade
        paperback) | ISBN 9781984857576 (ebook)
    Subjects: LCSH: Career development. | Job hunting. |
        College majors. | Employment interviewing.
    Classification: LCC HF5381 .B664 2021 | DDC 650.14--dc23
    LC record available at https://lccn.loc.gov/2020042838

Trade Paperback ISBN: 978-1-9848-5756-9
eBook ISBN: 978-1-9848-5757-6

Printed in the United States of America

Acquiring editor: Lisa Westmoreland | Editor: Ashley Pierce
Designer: Lauren Rosenberg | Production manager: Dan Myers
Copyeditor: Andrea Chesman | Proofreader: Meisha Mayo
Indexer: Ken DellaPenta
Publicist: Lauren Kretzchmar | Marketer: Monica Stanton

The icons on page 9 by Laurin Kraan, Komkrit Noenpoempisut,
iconcheese, ProSymbols, and Made by Made, respectively. The icons
on page 99 by Gregory Montigny, Azam Ishaq, Tippawan Sookruay, and
Smalllike, respectively. The icons on page 191 by Prettycons,
P Phanga Vignesh, Komkrit Noenpoempisut, and Tippawan Sookruay,
from thenounproject.com.

10 9 8 7 6 5 4 3 2 1

First Edition